HOW TO IMPROVE YOUR SEA FISHING

HOW TO IMPROVE YOUR SEA FISHING
Melvyn Bagnall

MACDONALD AND JANE'S · LONDON

© Melvyn Bagnall 1978
First published in 1976 by Queen Anne Press Limited
Jacket photography: Studio Glynde
Jacket design: Judy Tuke
Line drawings: Roy Schofield
Black and white photographs: Bill Goddard

All rights reserved. This book is sold subject to the condition that it shall not, by way of trade or otherwise, be lent, re-sold, hired out, or otherwise circulated without the publisher's prior consent in any form of binding or cover other than that in which it is published and without a similar condition including this condition being imposed on the subsequent purchaser. No part of this publication may be reproduced, stored in a retrieval system, or transmitted in any form or by any means electrical, mechanical, photocopied, recorded, or otherwise without the prior permission of the publisher.

ISBN 0354 08530 1

Published by Macdonald and Jane's Publishers Limited,
Paulton House, 8 Shepherdess Walk, London, N1 7LW
Printed in Great Britain by Hazell Watson & Viney Limited,
Aylesbury, Bucks.

Contents

Cod	7
Whiting	18
Bass	20
Mullet	30
Wrasse	37
Flounder	47
Soles	52
Dabs	54
Mackerel	57
Plaice	62
Haddock	67
Turbot and brill	72
Bream	77
Tope	83
Dogfish	88
Shark	90
Conger	97
Coalfish and pollack	105
Ling	109
Skates and rays	111
Halibut	122
Pouting	126

Cod

The cod is, without doubt, the most sought-after fish found around the British Isles. Scores of thousands of anglers fish for cod, mainly in the autumn to early spring period when the fish move inshore along vast sections of the coast. Early October usually sees the start of this cod fishing festival. The fish move in from deeper water as the temperature begins to drop and, if the season proves to be a good one, fish will be landed along more than half the British shoreline. The cod move into some Dorset and all Sussex and Kent coasts. They move up the Thames estuary and are found all the way north from East Anglia to the border and beyond. On the western shoreline they show on the North Devon and Somerset coasts, around all of Wales and northwards to Lancashire, Cumbria, and the Scottish coast.

The quality of each cod season depends largely for its success on the quality of the preceding cod hatches. Heavy commercial fishing around the coasts severely slashes stocks but three years after a good hatch – and the quality of the annual hatch varies immensely – sport can be very good indeed. Cod fishing reached a hitherto untouched peak in the mid-1960s. The arrival in anglers' hands of better fishing tackle – superior multiplier reels and casting rods – allowed the average angler to cast better and therefore to catch many more fish. The result was a cod fishing boom.

Individual catches of 10 fish to each tide became commonplace and there are examples of anglers catching more than 50 cod each from the shore during this peak period. That many of these fish were small codling of 1 lb to 3 lb mattered little. The calibre of the sport and the certainty that fish would be caught kept the popular beaches constantly topped up with anglers. The British cod record, which had stood at 32 lb since 1945, tumbled time after time until today it stands at what would once have been considered meteoric heights. George Martin caught the record fish in South Devon waters in 1972. It weighed 53 lb, but even this giant fish can be beaten. Trawlermen have landed cod of over 60 lb from British inshore waters. This, incidentally, is the current boat-caught record. The shore record stands at 44½ lb, a fish caught by B. Jones at Toms Point, Barry, Glamorgan.

The cod boom which began in earnest in the 1960s spread to boat fishing and, with the location of some staggeringly successful cod marks in the Firth of Clyde, the months of January and February in particular began to produce 40-pounders with regularity. Offshore wreck marks in the English Channel became stocked up with cod, it is believed for the first time. The Isle of Wight and sections of Dorset coast also began to produce cod. In 1975 a 31-pounder was taken from the shore in Devon – an event which would at one time have been thought impossible.

The great snag with a peak stock is that ultimately it has to decline and decline it did. The 1974 cod season began well enough with a good showing of biggish fish along the popular shorelines of Kent, Sussex, and East Anglia. But by December the fishing had tailed off badly and, although a few small spring fish arrived in early March, the season was disappointing. Cumberland, Wales, and the south coast fished badly, but oddly enough, the Yorkshire, Northumberland, and Durham sections reached a new peak with quality catches being reported regularly throughout the winter.

Long term, the prospects were not so bright. The 1974 cod hatch has been suggested by Ministry scientists to be very large indeed, and that offers hope. But the biggish hatches of three and four years earlier suffered 75 per cent losses in three years as the result of heavy trawling. The member nations of the North East Atlantic Fisheries Commission have been advised by marine scientists that over-fishing is a great threat to cod stocks, among others. As a result a limit was imposed on cod catches from the North Sea in 1975. The ceiling was set at a quarter of a million tons, but there is good reason for thinking this was too high a total, probably an unattainable total – even if the trawlers fished to maximum capacity. However, the situation looked brighter, if only temporarily, during the 1977/78 season when the North Sea was fairly alive with codling.

Restrictions on trawling in Icelandic and other distant waters have led to increased pressure on North Sea stocks and there is a clear danger that cod will be fished to near extinction – as happened with haddock in the north-west Atlantic. At present commercial fishing is a free-for-all with all nations happily taking cod from the sea before the fish have had time to grow to a size at which it makes economic sense to kill them. If cod were allowed to live until they were six years old they would weigh between 10 and 15 lb. But the majority are taken at three years when they weigh only 3 lb to 6 lb. This clearly illustrates that the seas are not being adequately farmed for their cod crop. If there is any consolation in this for anglers it must be that in the very near future the trawling industry will fish itself out of existence. Twentieth century logic should be capable of preventing such a calamity but it is right to point out that cod fishing is in some danger.

SHORE FISHING

For most of the year the stocks of cod stay far from shore but they begin their inshore movement in September. Shore fishing prospects for cod depend on a number of important factors and anglers who take these into account will always obtain the best results. Shore fishing is infinitely better in the dark hours. Cod move much closer to land at night, probably because only then do they feel safe to do so. Shore anglers can catch two cod at night for every one taken in daylight. Only a small proportion of Britain's cod anglers are prepared to give up a full night's sleep to maintain a dusk to dawn vigil over their cod rods. But hundreds do that every weekend when the season is in full swing, braving snow, and frost in the process.

Tides are important. The effect of tides tend to vary in relation to the shape and length of each beach but as a general rule the period around high water is considered best in most places. That is not to say that cod cannot be caught either at low water or even on ebb tides. Of course they can, but it does pay to ask for local advice before committing oneself to fish a particular tide. Periods of still, clear water produce poor results. Onshore gales quickly put colour into the sea and, although the sea may be too rough for fishing at such times, anglers can take immediate advantage once the wind dies away. Prospects remain good for as long as the water colour lasts.

Frost is also helpful. The fall in temperature seems to prompt fish to move inshore. Early frosts are welcomed for another reason by most anglers. The reduced water temperature sends the crabs scuttling off out to sea – where they are out of casting range and will not then be able to steal the bait from anglers' hooks.

Dead water times, when the sea is standing between tides, are usually less productive. The peak times are immediately before and immediately after high water.

Tackle

There is some controversy about fishing reels but little about the best rods for cod fishing. It is widely accepted that an ideal cod rod is 11 feet 6 inches long, weighs no more than 30 oz, and possesses what is known as a fast taper. This means that the glass fibre blanks from which the rod is made have a stepped-down diameter to provide a tip-action. The tip-action has two advantages. It helps the caster 'feel' his lead while he is in the motions of casting and the softish rod top gives better bite indications than a stiff top.

Just as it is possible to pay up to £45 for a good cod rod, so good quality reels can be equally expensive, if you insist on a multiplier reel. On the basis that the cheapest is rarely, if ever, the best, most experienced cod anglers tend to opt for better quality reels. Multipliers, as opposed to fixed-spool reels, are the most highly rated. They need to have plastic, not metal spools, to ensure that the reels rate of spin slows towards the end of the cast. If the reel continues to rotate at speed, throwing off more line than the lead is consuming on passage out to sea, an over-run can result. This means a bird's-nest type tangle will follow, and that could mean the angler loses as much as 30 minutes fishing time while he unravels the muddle.

A good multiplier has a narrow drum for this too helps the cast. The reel throws off less line towards the conclusion of each cast simply because the length of line required to complete a full turn of the spindle is much reduced as the reel empties. This, in turn, helps mitigate against over-runs (see figure 1).

The fixed-spool reel is widely rated the easiest reel to cast with; certainly for beginners to use. In a comparatively short time anglers can cast 60 to 70 yards and there is less risk of the constant tangles that can dog the progress of an inexperienced multiplier reel user. The biggest snag with fixed-spool reels is that manufacturers have so far declined to make a really outstanding model, comparable in quality to the best multipliers. If they did, opinion is that the fixed-spool would then equal the multiplier in performance. But such a reel would be expensive and manufacturers have some doubt that this would prove a viable commercial proposition. The spool of a fixed-spool reel should be filled with line to within an eighth of an inch of the lip for best results. This helps minimise friction as the line leaves the spool and passes upward through the rod rings.

Casting can be a painful experience for those who press for maximum distance. The index finger is used to lock the line and prevent it leaving the spool while the rod is being compressed just prior to the cast. Ideally, a finger stall should be worn to prevent cuts and bruises from the pressure of the line. A number of patent devices have been marketed. The 'thumb button' is one, which enables the line to be held in position by mechanical

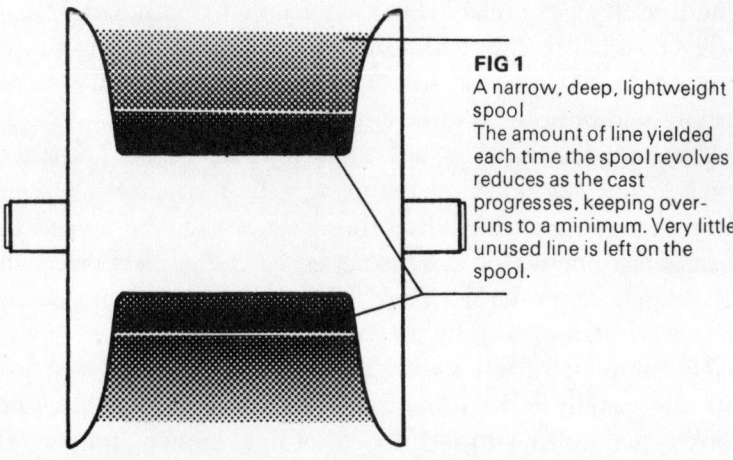

FIG 1
A narrow, deep, lightweight spool
The amount of line yielded each time the spool revolves reduces as the cast progresses, keeping over-runs to a minimum. Very little unused line is left on the spool.

means rather than with the finger. This takes much of the potential agony out of fixed-spool casting.

Thick line handicaps casting. The thicker the line the shorter the distance which can be cast. Cod anglers are keen to reduce the breaking strain, and thereby the diameter, of the lines they use simply to achieve maximum casting range. There is little doubt that the angler who is capable of casting baited tackle 100 yards and more from shore will catch more than his share of the cod. So the majority settle for nylon monofilament line with a breaking strain of around 18 lb. Only on the north-east coast of England, where fishing tends to be into rock gullies, where line suffers from abrasion and subsequent loss of strength, is thicker line necessary. In those places a 25 lb breaking strain is popular with the local anglers who, in any case, do not need to cast so far to reach the cod as men fishing from more open beaches.

Distance casting demands that a casting leader is used. This is a length of stronger line which takes the stress of the casting. Ideally it has a breaking strain of 35 lb to 45 lb. A casting leader should have three turns around the reel spool while running the length of the rod to the link swivel which connects either to the paternoster or lead. This means it needs to be around 16 feet to 18 feet in length. The casting leader is tied to the main reel line with a five-turn bloodknot (see figure 2a).

A 6 oz lead is most commonly used, although there is one school of thought which takes the view that 5 oz is better. It is rarely possible to fish with leads lighter than 4 oz because of strong tides. At times it may even be necessary to use 8 oz of lead to hold bottom. But the 6 oz is the easiest to cast.

Long range casting demands simple terminal tackle. The more cumbersome the hook rig the greater the resistance it creates during the cast and the shorter the distance it will be propelled. That is just one reason why experienced cod anglers prefer to fish with a single hook. They believe that there is no better chance of catching a cod with two hooks anyway.

The simplest rig involves a three-way swivel which is tied into the casting leader some three feet above the weight. The hook is tied on to a 10-inch length of line, known as a snood, which in turn is tied to the three-way swivel with a bloodknot (see figure 2b).

The angler's choice of hooks varies widely. Sharp, slim shanked hooks sizes 4/0 and 5/0 are favoured along the east coast, but when big cod are around it can be safest to fish a 6/0 or even a bigger one. Size 2/0 hooks can be very effective for small cod and whiting, but they have often been known to fail when hooked into big cod.

Baits
The primary bait is the lugworm, although ragworm and peeler crab will also prove effective. When fishing lugworm it usually pays to thread sufficient worms on to the hook to provide a bait which is up to nine inches long. The worms should be changed every 20 minutes to ensure that they continue to emit their pungent juices to the sea, thus helping to attract the cod.

Methods
There are many varied casting styles in operation today. The pendulum style is the most spectacular. It involves, as the name implies, swinging the lead to and fro until the rod is under maximum compression from the lead. At that point the cast is executed with the lead passing over the caster's head and far out to sea. This style is very popular with tournament casters and the most skilful of its exponents can cast baited tackle 150 yards.

The layback is a simple style. This involves the angler extending the rod tip as far up the beach behind him as possible. The lead is 'dropped' to secure compression of the tip and then the cast gets underway with the rod tip passing over the angler's shoulder at the 11 o'clock position. The lead is not flung idly out to sea. The angler must place the lead in an uptide position so that it settles on to the sea bed anything from 10 yards uptide to square with the spot where he is standing.

If the lead is either cast or carried downtide it will be dragged inshore and valuable distance will be lost. And because of the amount of 'belly' in the line it is always much more difficult to strike and hook a cod from the downtide position. The wire prongs on the casting lead can only get a fast bite into the sea

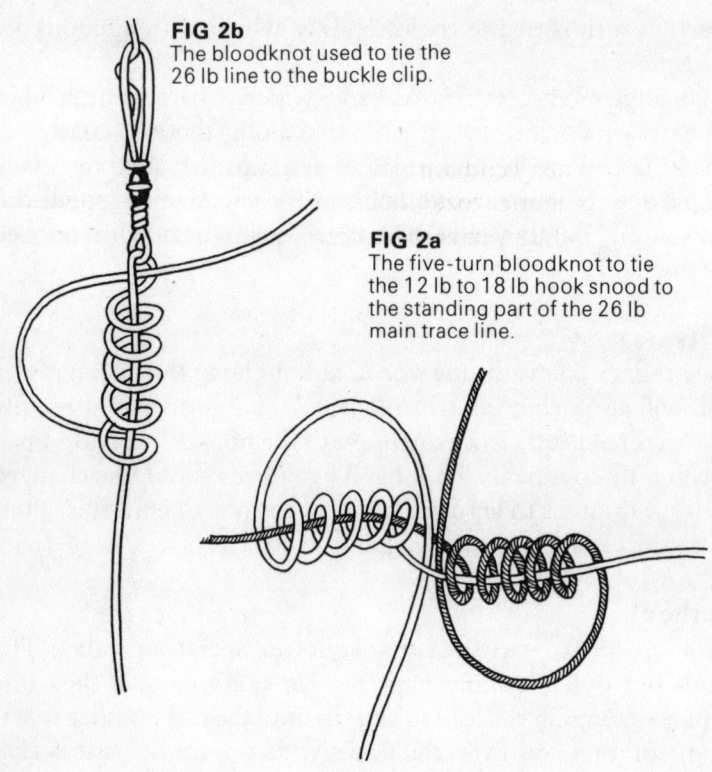

FIG 2b
The bloodknot used to tie the 26 lb line to the buckle clip.

FIG 2a
The five-turn bloodknot to tie the 12 lb to 18 lb hook snood to the standing part of the 26 lb main trace line.

bed if the line is left slack immediately after the cast has been made. The line can be tightened once the lead grips the bottom but not before (see figure 3).

The best leads in general use these days are called 'breakaway' leads. The wire prongs rotate backwards under pressure from the rod to allow them to pull cleanly out of the sand when the weight is to be retrieved. These leads also have the advantage that they do not foul bottom during the retrieve or when a fish is being brought through the breakers.

Given the time to do so, cod will frequently hook themselves. It is, in fact, better to give cod too much time rather than too little. As they take the bait and tug they pull against the lead weight gripped into the sea bed and hook themselves. Hooked fish are allowed to swim inshore with as little pressure from the rod as possible. A big fish is likely to put up good resistance

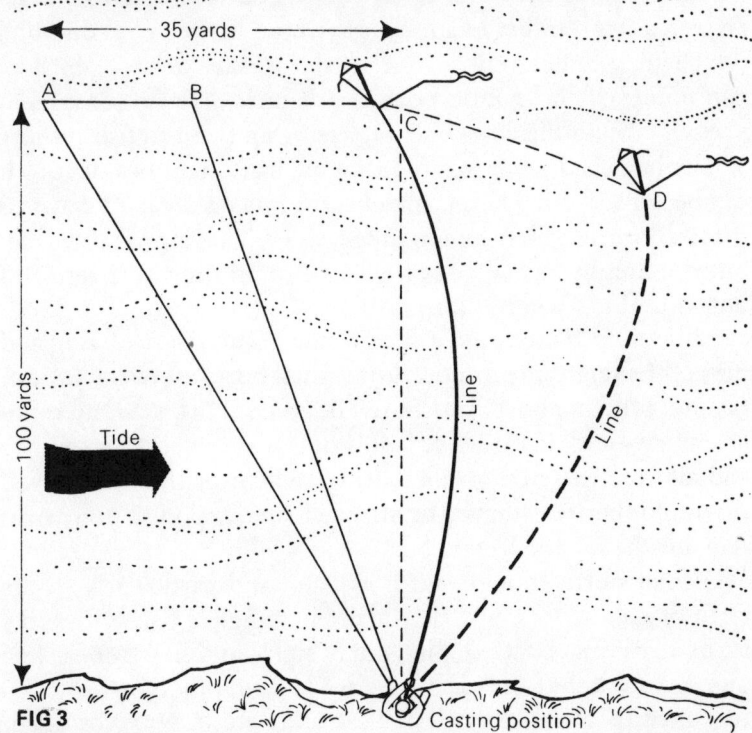

FIG 3

when just beyond the breakers and it is best to let the fish tire in the open sea rather than let it display its energies when being brought into a breaker. Fish should be brought up the beach on the crest of a wave. The inward power of the wave will fling the fish up the beach, and when the water has receded, leave the cod almost high and dry.

Any 10 lb cod from the shore is a good fish. A 20-pounder is outstanding and 30-pounders are very rare. But since Sam Hook's 32 lb record fish was first beaten in the mid-1960s several dozen cod weighing more than 30 lb have been caught from the shore. The biggest to date is the 44½-pounder taken from the South Wales shoreline at Barry by Brandon Jones.

BOAT FISHING

As the result of the build-up in cod catches in the last 10 years an increasing number of anglers have bought their own dinghies which they either trail by car to the seaside or store in boat compounds. These little boats are launched from convenient sites all around the coast and anglers using them to fish inshore waters have had great fun and caught large quantities of cod. It can be argued that a beach angler earns his cod the hard way and that inshore dinghy fishing is much easier. That is probably true, but the dinghy fisher loses a lot of fishing time as a result of unfavourable sea conditions.

All around the east, south east, and south coast of England the cod fishing done inshore from small boats involves bottom fishing, with the boat at anchor. The rod is short – casting is not necessary – and, because the bait is simply dropped over the side and allowed to settle on the bottom wherever the tide allows, the multiplier reels have the stronger metal spools. Lugworm remains the most effective bait.

Further north though, into Scotland and particularly in the Firth of Clyde hotspots, the small boat anglers fish with pirks from a drifting boat. A pirk can weigh anything from a few ounces to 2 lb but the ideal weight for Firth of Clyde fishing is reckoned to weigh 7 oz. The best pirks are heavily chromed, which explains the popularity of car door handles as cheap substitutes. The lure is allowed to reach bottom and is then lifted and allowed to rise and fall in the water. Most fish are usually taken in the lower three to four fathoms. Drift fishing allows the angler to cover substantial areas of water – and also helps the effective fishing of the pirk, since both boat and pirk are being carried away downstream with the flow together. This is the method which has produced a spate of 40 lb-plus cod from famous Gantocks mark, off Dunoon.

There are some areas, notably the north-east coast of England and the sea lochs on Scotland's west coast, where cod remain inshore through the summer. There are barely enough fish to provide worthwhile sport in most of these places, but no one need be surprised if he catches a cod there in summer.

The remarkable increase in sea angling from boats – this is

predicted to be the fastest growing aspect of angling – has resulted in cod being caught in what were once quite unexpected places. Offshore wrecks as much as 40 miles from land, some of these located mid-way between England and France, have yielded fine catches of cod throughout the summer months. As a general rule is seems to be true that, the further offshore the wreck is situated, the better the chance that it contains quantities of cod. The cod mix in with shoals of pollack and coalfish and are therefore virtually impossible to fish for exclusively.

Drift fishing with any of the variety of imitation sand-eels now available is always likely to produce cod – and they can be big fish. It is very rare for cod taken off wreck marks to weigh less than 14 lb, and many top 20 lb. It was from an offshore wreck that George Martin caught his 53 lb record-breaker. That was the captor's first-ever day of boat fishing. He was talked into going by friends, was not at all keen, caught the biggest cod to date, and refused to be at all overawed by his fish!

Wreck cod are taken deep down in the water, frequently at depths of 200 feet or more. The imitation sand-eel lures are fished on a long lead-free trace which allows them to be carried around in the tide and thereby presented attractively to the fish.

At one time deep sea anglers fishing wrecks used to fish as many as three lures at once and, such is the concentration of fish on some of these wrecks, they quite frequently hooked three big fish simultaneously. The result was chaos. An excessive amount of expensive tackle was lost and it was found that lines of up to 70 lb breaking strain had to be used if the anglers were to have any chance of landing a trio of fish at one haul. More recently the wreck fishermen have become reconciled to single-lure fishing (see figure 4) but because of the depths of water, the strength of the offshore tides and the power of fight from the fish it is not possible to use line of less than 40 lb breaking strain.

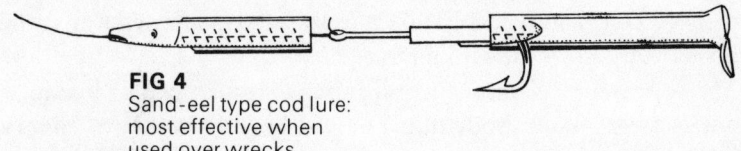

FIG 4
Sand-eel type cod lure:
most effective when
used over wrecks.

Whiting

The first frosts herald the 'official' arrival of the whiting, one of our most abundant and co-operative fish. Due to the fact that whiting are small compared with other winter species such as haddock and cod they are regarded as somewhat inferior by many anglers. But very often it is a case of people using the wrong tackle. Almost every species of fish has certain sporting qualities if it is fished for in the correct way. Whiting, like many other of our smaller fish, suffer from the fact that they are usually caught on tackle designed for bigger species – in this case cod.

Distribution
More southern in their availability than cod and haddock, whiting are hardy little fish. They have warded off the threat of commercial fishing better than most other fish, mainly because of their fast growth rate and because they reach maturity early. They prefer areas of clean sea bed, usually of a sandy or muddy nature, and are found in water from five to 50 fathoms deep – though it is normally the smaller fish which are found in the shallows.

During the summer whiting stay in the deep, cooler water offshore. They arrive inshore during November and filter away again in about the middle of February prior to spawning. They are normally the last of the winter residents in British waters. They are most common in the Channel and the North Sea where fish taken on rod and line average 1 lb to 2 lb. S. Dearman established the present British boat-caught record with a 6¼ lb fish taken in West Bay, Dorset, in 1977. The shore-caught best of 3 lb 2 oz was set up by C. T. Kochevar at Dungeness, Kent, in 1976. But fish over 8 lb taken in trawl nets are proof that the record is by no means invincible.

In appearance, whiting are slimmer fish than cod or haddock with a streamlined body and pointed head. They have silvery flanks and a greeny, brown back with a conspicuous dark spot just in front of the shoulders. Whiting move in large shoals and generally feed close to the bottom. The natural diet of the smaller fish consists of worms, sand-eels, shrimps, and crabs, though the bigger fish are more predatory and will also take small whiting, small pouting, herring fry, pilchards, and sprats. The whiting's mouth is full of sharp teeth and the angler must be careful when unhooking his catch. Competition anglers have been known to shred their fingers badly when catching whiting in large numbers.

Tackle and methods
The best way to gain maximum sport from whiting fishing is to catch them from a boat. Beach fishing requires heavier tackle for casting and this rules out the fishing qualities of the whiting. A light two-hook paternoster is an ideal terminal rig when boat fishing and should be combined with a light eight-foot hollow glass boat rod, a small multiplier reel loaded with 10 lb line and a weight of not more than 2 oz when possible. A fish, which has a heavy weight to drag around, is not going to be much of a sporting proposition.

Whiting can be caught readily during the day in 10 fathoms of water or more. But they feed far better in the dark, and especially when it is frosty, they will venture close inshore. This is when they are best caught from the beach, again on a light paternoster. Pier fishing is also productive. Whiting can usually be found among the cod shoals when fishing from both boat and shore and it is common to get a good fish on a big bait intended for cod.

Baits
The choice of whiting baits is wide. Fish strips are good and many beach-caught whiting are taken on lugworm. Sprat and squid are particularly successful baits for big whiting found towards the western end of the Channel. Make sure the bait is well hooked, for otherwise whiting will soon remove it or shred it with their sharp teeth. When they take the bait properly, whiting produce a good knock on the rod top and a spirited fight on the tackle described. Whiting are a highly-rated table fish, but do not keep for long, so they are at their best when eaten fresh.

Bass

Big, bold, and beautiful . . . that's the bass, a splendidly handsome fish which is extremely highly rated for its sporting qualities. It has just about everything in its favour from the angling viewpoint: it is fairly well distributed around our coasts; it grows to a weight of over 20 lb; it can be caught by a number of different methods from both boat and shore; it fights remarkably well; and it is usually good to eat.

So popular is the bass, that a special society devoted to fishing for them was formed in 1973. This body, which also works for the conservation of bass, is known as the Bass Anglers Sportfishing Society – BASS in short. The Society already has over 400 members and its strength is fast increasing. The secretary is Jim Churchouse, Rishon, Longfield Road, Weymouth, Dorset.

The bass has an almost noble appearance. A member of the sea perch family, it is a muscular yet streamlined fish. It is covered in big silvery scales and has a spiney first dorsal fin – there are two – and spiney gill covers. Its armour-like back is usually varying shades of grey, but can be green and is sometimes a dusky blue in the larger specimens. The belly is white and the mouth very large. All in all the bass is really something special.

Very small bass – fish under 2 lb or so – are commonly known as school bass. But bass generally average from 2 lb to 6 lb and while double-figure fish can be regarded as specimens they are not uncommon. The British record of 18 lb 6 oz was caught over the Eddystone Reef, a very prolific bass mark off Plymouth, in 1975, by R. G. Slater. The previous record, an 18 lb 2 oz fish caught by F. C. Borley at Felixstowe, is still the best from the shore. But bass to nearly 30 lb have been captured in the nets of commercial fishermen.

Distribution

Bass are basically found in the southern waters of the British Isles though they do occur at intervals in northern waters. They are most common along the south west and Channel coasts of England and the west and south coasts of Ireland. The Welsh coast is fairly good bass ground, particularly in the south where the Gower Peninsula is celebrated bass territory. A number of big bass fishing competitions are held in Wales each year.

Bass are fairly common in the Irish Sea as far north as the Mersey estuary and in the North Sea as far north as Spurn Head. But only the occasional small fish is caught along the north east coast and they are comparatively rare in Scottish waters. The occasional very big fish is taken in the north of Ireland, the 16 lb 6 oz specimen landed by Jim McClelland on the Causeway Coast at Castlerock being a typical example. That fish, taken in November 1972, is the Irish record.

Bass are very active fish and feed at varying levels in the water. Their favourite haunts include estuaries and river mouths, lagoons and muddy creeks. West Country estuaries such as the Teign, Fowey, Dart, and Exe are particularly good for bass fishing. They will also ascend rivers for some distance but do not often penetrate freshwater. On the beaches they prefer mixed ground of sand and rocks, the weed-covered rocks providing plenty of food. Bass are predatory fish and they like to lurk in the rocks before ambushing their prey in the gullies. This type of ground is especially good for big fish.

As explained earlier bass can be caught from both boat and beach. They venture right inshore to feed in the surf and also thrive over offshore reefs. The Eddystone Reef off Plymouth is a typical example of a good bass reef. Plymouth policeman Spencer Vibart is famous for the superb catches of big bass he has taken from this mark on artificial sand-eels. His best fish to date is a 14 lb 4½ oz specimen caught in November 1974.

Bass could never be accused of being fussy eaters. In some harbours they will feed largely on offal and supplement that diet only with worms and crustaceans. Generally speaking, however, school bass feed chiefly on small crustaceans like shrimps, as well as worms, sand-eels and on the small fry of species such as herring and mullet. Bigger bass are more predatory and their diet is made up mainly of sprats, herring, pilchard fry, and sand-eels. Small flatfish will also be included in the diet of bass feeding over sandy ground.

This species often group together in massive shoals when feeding in earnest. They drive the shoals of fry to the surface and dash around in pursuit of their prey, causing a disturbance on the surface of the water. This splashing, together with the sight of the spiney dorsal fins, will reveal the existence of bass to the angler. The presence of sea birds, which quickly gather overhead to get their share of the fry, will also help the angler locate feeding bass.

From the seasonal aspect, bass are basically a summer species. They arrive inshore in the spring, the time varying according to the locality. They may crop up in some areas as early as February, but they do not appear until mid-April in most places. The rapid cooling-off of shallow inshore waters soon leads to the winter offshore movement of bass. This is usually in October, though they sometimes delay migration until mid-November. Again this depends on locality. They can still be caught in the deeper offshore waters during mild winters, particularly in the West Country. Strangely enough the mid-summer months of July and August are not the best months for catching bass. Most experts prefer May, June, and September; and October can often offer excellent late season sport.

It would be a crime to discuss the bass without stressing the necessity for conservation, for they have been hit harder than most species by overfishing – and not just the commercial fishermen are to blame. Greedy anglers have also done their share of damage by killing large numbers which they cannot possibly dispose of. Bass are not fast-growing and anglers who kill them, especially the smaller fish, are ruining their future sport. Once an angler has caught sufficient fish for his purposes he should return any surplus to the water. The National Federation of Sea Anglers have long been pressing the Ministry of Agriculture, Fisheries, and Food to introduce a size limit for bass. The Federation's aim is to make it illegal for bass under 14 inches to be removed from the water. But at the time of writing there was still considerable indignation among sea anglers that the Ministry should see fit to continue with the inadequate 10-inch limit. Bass of this size will not have reached spawning maturity and will not have spawned even once before they die.

Methods

Spinning
This is the most sporting and exciting method of catching bass and results in the capture of more fish than any other approach. It is most effective when used from a boat but will also take fish from rocks, estuaries, piers, jetties, and, to a lesser extent, from the beaches.

The great advantage of spinning is that it allows the use of light tackle. A nine- or 10-foot carp rod is ideal, though many anglers use rods designed for salmon spinning. The reel should be of the fixed-spool variety, preferably with a fast retrieve, and the line can be as light as 8 lb for boat fishing. Spinning from the rocks requires a slightly heavier line because of the risk of becoming snagged in rocks or weed. A 12 lb line is more suitable in this department therefore. Wire traces are not necessary when fishing for bass but an 18-inch nylon trace of equal breaking strain to the reel line should be used. This should have a link swivel at one end to clip on to the bait and a normal barrel swivel at the other to attach the trace to the reel line. Keep the swivels oiled and free running to prevent kinking of the line.

Choice of lures is wide. A silver spoon about four inches long is an excellent lure and the well-known Toby spoon is a favourite with bass anglers. But half the fun of spinning is selecting a lure and there are many, many more which will take bass. It is often a case of matching up the spoon to the size of fish the bass happen to be feeding on at the time. If sprats are the quarry then a four-inch silver lure is fine. But, if the bass are chasing something much smaller, then a lure of two inches or less may do the trick. The choice of lure also depends on the depth of water being fished and at what level the bass are feeding. A light lure is best for fishing in shallow water or for catching bass near the surface, but a heavy lure is obviously better for fishing deep water.

Weight can be added to a lure to help it sink faster, but it often detracts from the action of the lure and, in any case, defeats the object of fishing light.

Spinning for bass often appeals to the freshwater angler and his collection of spinners and plugs for pike fishing can come in useful. Few anglers use plugs for bass fishing and there is room for experimentation in this field. Bass have been taken on plugs, though few anglers use them consistently enough for any conclusions to be formed about their effectiveness. There are many different types of plug. Some are called 'floaters' which dance and plop on the surface as they are retrieved. Others are known as 'divers' and are equipped with a diving vane which cuts under the water and forces the plug below the surface as it is wound in. There must be certain patterns among the scores of different types of plug which would take bass consistently.

Spinning and plug fishing are not just cases of casting and retrieving lures. The angler can improve the action of his lure by his use of the rod and reel. Try the 'quick, quick, slow' style of retrieve – winding the reel very fast and then slowing down or stopping altogether, allowing the lure to falter or fall temptingly through the water. Alternatively try moving the rod from side to side as you retrieve, causing the lure to carve crazy, wavy patterns in the water. The bass is a curious fish and these actions may provoke it to strike. Similarly, when a bass is in a finicky mood a fish strip on the treble hook of the lure may tempt it.

A good general rule is to retrieve the lure very quickly, hence the fast retrieve reel. Do not worry about the bass. They are one of the fastest movers in the sea and, if they want to catch your lure, they will.

Though not a spinner in the true sense of the word, a rubber eel of the type used to catch pollack and coalfish has emerged as an excellent bass lure. It can be jigged or trolled. Another way of taking bass is the 'sink and draw' method. This involves the angler making several turns of the reel while lifting the rod at the same time. The effect is to draw the rubber eel up through the water fairly rapidly. The angler then stops reeling and drops his rod, allowing the lure to flutter lifelessly down through the water. This action is particularly effective for catching a number of species, the bass included. The fish may take as the lure is being drawn up through the water or as it falls.

Spinning for bass from a boat is fairly easy fishing. A feeding shoal can often be located by their splashing or by the whirling sea-birds overhead and since the bait is not being presented on the bottom there is little danger of the line becoming snagged. Rock fishing is a different proposition. As well as the problem of lost tackle, the angler also has the task of steering hooked fish clear of the snags. It is an advantage, therefore, to know the ground you are fishing. When you have decided where you are going to fish take the opportunity of inspecting the area at low water to get the lie of the land and the likely bass spots. Rocky headlands are good places for bass fishing, despite the risk of losing tackle. They like the rough water and the strong tide races familiar with these areas. The best state of the tide for bass fishing is usually when it is at its fastest. This does, however, depend on the locality and a good time in one place may not be so good in another.

A word of warning to anglers buying lures from tackle shops. The treble hooks are almost always too small and are usually not sharp enough. Replace them with larger ones and sharpen them yourself. It pays to carry a small sharpening stone with your tackle when fishing over rugged ground, for hooks will soon lose their sharpness on the rocks.

Bottom fishing on rough ground

Spinning may be the most exciting method of catching bass, but legering over rough ground from the shore is the method most likely to turn up really big fish. Rough ground is the general name given to a mixture of rocks and sand – small areas of sand punctuated with low-lying rocks or sandwiched in rocky gullies. They are not easy to fish and tackle losses are inevitable among the weed and rocks. But this is where the big, solitary bass roam, feeding on the wealth of crustaceans, eels, and small fish in the rocks and ambushing fish in the gullies.

The aim is to put your bait on the sandy patches. As explained above, it is a great advantage to carry out a survey of the ground to be fished at low water. Some anglers mark the sandy patches, using balloons as buoys. Accurate casting is essential. For once the bait has hit the bottom it must be left alone. Try reeling it into another spot and it will almost certainly become snagged in the rocks.

The terminal tackle – a simple paternoster – is designed with rough ground in mind. The weight is attached to the rig via a 'rotten bottom', i.e. a length of nylon of lower breaking strain than the reel line. Then, in the event of the weight becoming snagged, the angler pulls for a break and only the weight is lost. The tackle is made up by a light beachcaster and a multiplier loaded with 20 lb line. A one-hook paternoster minimises the chances of the tackle getting snagged but two hooks can be used when the angler knows the ground well.

Crab is the supreme bait for this type of fishing, peeler and soft crabs being preferred to hardbacks. It must be explained that crabs change their shells during the year. It is in the early stages of this process – when the shell splits down the middle – that the crab is known as a peeler. When the old shell has gone and the new one is forming it is known as a soft crab. The crab then hardens up again. Hardback crabs are taken by bass if the crab is small, but the difficulty comes in mounting it on the hook, with the shell proving an obstacle.

Peeler and soft crabs are best used whole with the legs left on. Some anglers hook them once through the middle, while others prefer to pass the hook through the eye sockets. It is always a good precaution to secure the crab to the hook with elasticated cotton to make sure it stays on during the cast. The old shell should be removed from a peeler before it is used. Squid and fish strips can also be used to good effect with this method.

Despite their size, big bass are not the boldest of biters. The first sign of a bite may be no more than a slight pluck. This is also the sign to give the fish slack line. It will then move away with the bait and the hook should be set with a powerful strike over the shoulder. The rod should be held at all times.

Bottom fishing on beaches

Otherwise known as surfcasting, this is a specialised method of bass fishing which provides a unique form of excitement for the angler. As the term implies, it involves catching bass from the surf. The best surfcasting beaches, or storm beaches as they are also known, are those which face the prevailing south west winds. They shelve slowly so that the waves break some distance from the shoreline. The best ones are probably found on the west coast of Ireland.

Although these beaches appear to be barren, the gouging action of the surf on the sand stirs up plenty of foodlife such as sand-eels and small fish, which attract the bass. As the surf bundles this food inshore, so the bass follow. Understandably then, the best time to fish is at the beginning of an onshore blow after a calm spell or immediately after a big blow when the waves are beginning to subside. The idea is to place the bait right in the surf. This will involve a long cast if the surf is breaking way out at low water and a short cast if it is breaking close inshore at high water.

A powerful beachcaster capable of hurling a 4 oz weight up to 100 yards, but light enough to give the angler some sport with his fish, is the type of rod required. A multiplier loaded with 15 lb line completes the basic tackle but a 'shock leader' is also required. This is a short length of stronger line, possibly 30 lb breaking strain, attached to the end of the reel line to help it withstand the shock of punching out a heavy lead, otherwise it would probably crack off under the pressure.

A two-hook paternoster is the most popular type of terminal tackle for surfcasting. The weight should be between 2 oz and 4 oz, depending on the strength of the tide. The best baits are lugworm, ragworm, mackerel, and razorfish.

Unlike bass caught over rough ground, fish caught on a storm beach will produce a bold bite, with the fish frequently tearing off on a searing run. There is always the exception to the rule, however, and it pays to hold the rod at all times, feeling for a more delicate bite from a big fish. Fighting a big bass in the surf is one of the delights of sea fishing. The fish must be played out in deep water before any attempt is made to land it. A big, lively bass in shallow water can be just too hot to handle.

Float fishing

This method is best suited to rough ground, making it possible for the angler to suspend his bait clear of the snags. It is also used from piers and jetties. It could easily be carried out from boats but there is little necessity for it. The same type of rod used for bass spinning – a 10-foot carp or salmon spinning rod – is ideal and should be teamed with a fixed-spool or light multiplying reel loaded with a 12 lb line. The length of rod is quite important since it will be needed for casting, for picking up the line from the water on the strike and for playing a hooked fish away from the rocks at the angler's feet.

A sliding float rig is best so that deep water may be fished if necessary. A long cast is not necessary since the tide will carry the float out, covering a lot of ground as it goes. In this way the angler can search out likely looking holes and gullies in the rocks with little risk of the line becoming snagged.

A big, live ragworm is probably the best bait to use on a float rig, but there are a number of others which will catch fish. These include crabs, sand-eels, and also elvers, a bait used to good effect by anglers off areas of the Dorset coast. Prawns are also a good bait but are delicate and should be used on a smaller, fine wire hook to keep them alive as long as possible. All baits are better used alive.

Bass venture very close inshore over rocky ground so be prepared for a bite under your feet as well as further offshore. A landing net with a long handle is more efficient than a gaff and it also means fish can be returned alive. For the same reasons, a landing net should also be used when spinning.

Livebaiting and deadbaiting

Since the bass is a predatory fish, it follows that livebaiting should be an effective method. Small pouting, mackerel, and wrasse, along with a host of other small fish, will tempt bass, though it is wise to use a bait over the type of ground on which it is normally found. A bass which comes across a strange visitor to his territory may be put off rather than attracted.

Livebaits are best fished on a short trace, say four feet, to minimise the danger of them roaming too far afield and becoming snagged around some obstruction. They are fished on a size 4/0 hook passed through the root of the tail or the bottom lip.

A conventional legered deadbait is not a particularly effective method of catching bass, but a variation has proved very successful in the past few seasons. News of this new style of fishing first reached the ears of the angling press with a spate of double-figure bass from Dover Breakwater. The anglers catching the fish were using deadbaits, usually pouting, which they injected with air by using medical syringes. These baits, which were used on a lead-free line, floated up in the water and proved deadly for bass. This method has since proved effective along other parts of our coastline.

Mullet

The popularity of this species can be gauged from the fact that a National Mullet Club was formed early in 1975. The formation of the club was fitting, but long overdue, recognition of what is rated by some anglers to be the hardest fighting fish in the sea. Members of the club aim to dispel the popularly held theory that mullet are hard to catch, arguing that, since they are under very little pressure from commercial fishing and that they seem to possess a greater resistance to pollution and disease than other species, they must be a fish of the future.

There are three species of mullet, all known as grey mullet. The one of prime concern to anglers is, not surprisingly, the biggest – the thick-lipped grey mullet. This fish, which is also the most common around our shores, is regularly caught to weights of over 5 lb. The British record stands at 10 lb 1 oz, a boat-caught fish taken at Portland, Dorset, by P. C. Libby in 1952. By comparison, the record for the thin-lipped grey mullet stands at only 5 lb 11 oz (a shore-caught specimen by D. E. Knowles from the River Rother in Sussex), and a 3 lb fish can be regarded as quite a capture. The mullet family decrease in size to the golden grey mullet, the record for which is only 2 lb 10 oz (shore-caught). The red mullet is not considered to be a true mullet, although it is included on the record list at 3 lb 10 oz (shore-caught) and 3 lb 8 oz (boat-caught).

THICK-LIPPED GREY MULLET

Distribution
Although this fish is found fairly extensively around our coasts, the best rod and line returns occur along the south coast. The Sussex, Hampshire, Dorset, and Devon coastlines are all capable of producing fine sport. Fish over 3 lb are common, but anything over 5 lb can be regarded as good. Mullet are basically a

summer fish, their season running from April and May when they first appear close inshore, through the warm months until August or September.

There is no doubt that a certain percentage of mullet are hard to catch. These are the wild mullet, fish which stick strictly to their natural diet and are difficult to tempt with a bait. They feed by scooping in mouthfuls of mud, swallowing the organic matter, and spitting out the waste material such as sand or ejecting it via their gills. This organic matter consists mainly of plant remains and microscopic algae. Wild mullet also graze on the algae which form on underwater rocks and breakwaters or even on the hulls of boats. Unlike most other fish, the mullet rarely feeds on other fish or small animals.

It is the mullet which gather to feed on the offal around the outfalls of food-producing factories, or move close inshore to take scraps thrown into harbours from boats or by holidaymakers, which really provide the sport for anglers. Mullet usually swim in shoals and in the summer they can often be seen swimming around the pylons of piers and jetties, working along harbour walls or swimming around moored boats in search of scraps of food. They can also be found foraging among the effluent discharged into the sea from sewage outfalls. In his book, *The Sea Angler's Fishes*, Michael Kennedy conveniently names these fish the 'urban' mullet and refers to the wilder variety as 'rural' mullet.

Tackle and methods

It is significant that Mullet Club secretary Gerald Green is convinced that the biggest proportion of anglers likely to join the club will be freshwater fishing converts. For mullet fishing is the closest sea angling comes to the freshwater side of the sport. In fact, it is really a case of applying freshwater tactics to the sea.

An 11-foot hollow fibre-glass rod is ideal. This will help steer a hooked fish away from jutting rocks or jetty supports. It would spell disaster if the fish should get around them. A rod of this length is also better for striking than a short one. As we shall see later, mullet fishing usually means float fishing and a long rod is best for picking up line from the water on the strike – especially at a distance. Team this type of rod with a fixed-spool reel of the freshwater type. This makes casting easier and, provided it has a good slipping clutch, it will allow good control of a fighting fish. Line strength depends on the timidity of the mullet you are fishing for. Use a 6 lb line for bold biting mullet, but scale down to 4 lb when the fish are more reluctant to take a bait. It is dangerous to go lower than this because of the mullet's exceptional fighting qualities.

Float fishing is the most productive method of catching mullet. A tiny porcupine quill of the type used for catching roach from freshwater is perfect. The float should not need more than one shot to cock it in the water. It can be fixed to the line so that the bait is suspended at a certain depth in the water or a sliding float can be used (see figure 5). A sliding float comes in useful when a fixed float is set to a depth which makes casting difficult. A float fixed at eight feet, for example, may lead to the hook catching on the rocks or harbour wall behind, when you attempt to cast. But a sliding float is stopped by a piece of elastic band on the line which can be reeled through the rod rings, thus overcoming the problem. The outfit is completed by a size 10 freshwater hook. It may pay to scale down to a size 12 if the fish are timid, while a size 8 is a safer bet when bites are bold.

A piece of breadflake the size of a two-pence piece is by far the best bait. Squeeze it on the shank and bend of the hook, concealing the point but leaving it free to penetrate on the strike. The bread should be squeezed firmly enough to keep it on the hook during the cast. But if you pinch fresh bread too tightly it will become rubbery once in the water and can easily be pulled out of the fish's mouth without the hook finding a hold.

Groundbait is not essential when mullet fishing, but few serious mullet men would consider fishing without it. The most convenient and effective groundbait is again made from bread. Just soak a loaf of bread in water, then drain the excess water from the bucket before mashing the loaf into a pulp. Handfuls of the groundbait should be thrown into the spot where the angler intends to fish. It will spread into a creamy cloud on contact with the water, but, while it will attract the mullet, it will not satisfy their appetites. Dropped into the cloud of groundbait,

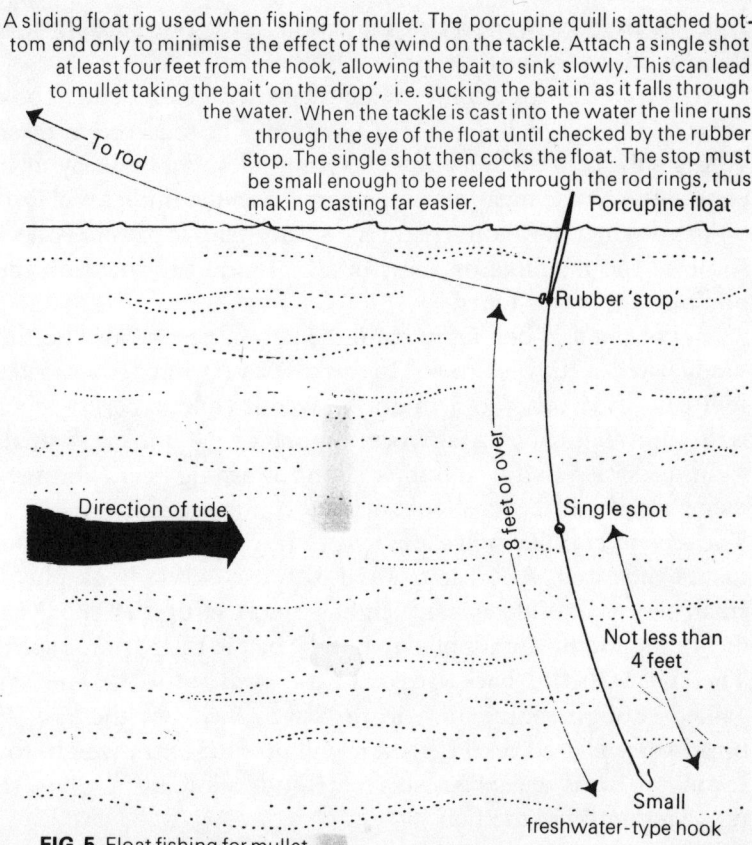

FIG 5 Float fishing for mullet.

the hookbait will appear as a bigger offering among the mashed morsels and fish seem particularly attracted to it. It is also evident when fishing in this fashion that there is some rivalry among the fish to get the bigger offering first. Pilchard oil is a groundbait additive used by some mullet experts, but it is not essential, especially in areas where mullet are known to feed.

Mullet can even be 'educated' to feeding on bread by a special groundbaiting technique. The idea is to groundbait the same spot each day so the mullet become used to feeding on bread. This is best done by leaving the bait on the rocks for the rising tide to wash off or to hang a carrot sack of mashed bread over a pier or harbour wall so that the action of the tide steadily sifts the cloud into the water.

Rocky coasts can often provide their own groundbait. Look for the gullies which dry out at low tide. The seaweed in these gullies will rot in the sun between spring tides. Flies will lay their eggs in the weed, maggots will emerge, and the mullet will feed on them when they come in on the spring tide. It pays to collect some of the maggots on these occasions and use them on the hook in threes and fours.

Mullet can also be caught from the beach, particularly on the sandy patches between rocks. In this case a very light paternoster will pay dividends and it might be worthwhile experimenting with the small tail of a ragworm on one of the hooks. A small swimfeeder is a useful addition to bottom fishing gear. The one-inch long plastic feeder should be light enough to roll in the tide. The sensitive mullet will soon detect a heavy swimfeeder or one that is anchored. Another method is to use only a hook plus a small shot – to add casting weight – two feet up the line. The fly casting method is adopted to put the bait in the required spot. The rod is flicked backwards and forwards until the line has gained enough momentum in the air to flick out the bait. If bread paste is used on the hook it will provide extra weight for casting. This is a very sensitive method, allowing the bait to move naturally in the tide.

Whatever method is used, the rod should be held at all times. The strike must be quick – there is no time for using rod rests or leaning the rod against pier railings. A landing net is essential, for you cannot lift fish out of the water on such small hooks and light line. This light tackle also makes it impossible to bully the fish to the net. Mullet are truly remarkable fighters. Their sleek bodies are built for speed and conceal an amazing amount of strength. Approach them in the right way and they will provide sporting qualities second to none.

THIN-LIPPED GREY MULLET
As mentioned earlier the British record for this member of the mullet family stands at 5 lb 11 oz, only just over half the record for its thick-lipped cousin. But there is positive evidence that the

fish grows to much greater proportions in British waters. For example, a 'monster' of 16 lb 12 oz was netted in Pagham Harbour, Sussex. There is little doubt, of course, that the thick-lipped species also grows to a much larger size than has been recorded on rod and line.

The two species are not easily definable by the untrained eye, though an expert has little difficulty in telling them apart. It is always worth checking the identity of the fish carefully, otherwise you may have a record on your hands without realising it. The most obvious difference between the two is, as their names suggest, in the lips – the upper lip being much more pronounced in the one than the other. There is also a noticeable difference in the dorsal fins. These – there are two – are smaller and wider apart in the thick-lipped mullet.

A crucial factor from the angler's viewpoint is that the thin-lipped variety is not so widely distributed. Almost all those recorded have come from the south and south-west coasts. The feeding habits of the two fish are similar. They also frequent the same haunts and are caught by similar angling techniques. Both thick- and thin-lipped mullet are often found in rivers well away from the sea. The Sussex Rother is probably the best venue in the country for freshwater mullet fishing.

GOLDEN GREY MULLET

This fish is distinguished by a conspicuous golden spot on the gill covers, much different from more poorly defined golden blotches found on the gill covers and flanks of the other two species of mullet. Its qualities as a sporting fish are dubious to say the least. For it is both a rare fish and a small one. The occasional golden grey mullet caught by anglers in British waters usually come from the Devon and Cornwall coastlines. The British shore-caught record of 2 lb 10 oz was caught at Burry Port, Wales, in 1976 by R. J. Hopkins. The boat-caught record of 1 lb ½ oz was caught in Southampton Water in 1977 by R. A. Andrews.

RED MULLET

This species is another of our rarer fish. As explained earlier, it is not a true mullet but belongs to an entirely different family known as *mullidae*. Found on parts of the south and south-west coasts of England and the south and west coasts of Ireland during the summer months, it is rarely caught by anglers and only then by accident. This small, attractive fish favours soft ground where it uses two long barbels beneath its chin to search out its food.

Wrasse

It is only in recent years that the humble wrasse has become recognised by anglers as a sporting fish. For traditionally this beautifully marked fish – a Cinderella among sea fish – was regarded merely as a scavenger which made a nuisance of itself by pinching baits intended for more 'noble' species such as bass. Few anglers fished for the wrasse seriously, mainly because the tough fish makes poor eating – a crucial factor years ago. But as attitudes changed and anglers began to catch fish more for the sport than for the pot so the wrasse began to come into its own. Anglers started to realise that the fish which smashed their tackle with powerful, searing runs were not massive conger but wrasse weighing as little as 4 lb and 5 lb. For there is no doubt that the wrasse, pound for pound, is among the hardest fighting fish in the sea . . . some would say it is the hardest.

The squat, bull-like appearance of the wrasse reflects its fighting character. Once hooked it takes a good angler and stout tackle to keep it from the weed and rocks among which it thrives. Basically a summer species, the wrasse is found in the gullies and crevices which penetrate the rockiest stretches of our coastline. Ironically it was the fish's preference for relatively shallow marks very close inshore which led to a massive depletion in stocks after the notorious winter of 1963.

Thousands of fish perished in those cruel arctic conditions. Piles of dead fish were washed up on our shores and a 5 lb wrasse was virtually unheard of during the next few summers. Before that dreadful winter the Cornish Federation of Anglers had imposed a minimum size list of 3 lb for the weighing-in of wrasse in their competitions – Cornwall being one of the country's most prolific areas for wrasse. But the measure became pointless after the freeze-up. Not even fish of that size were caught very often.

The lasting effect of the mass mortality is reflected by the chart which lists the biggest wrasse caught from 1963 to the spring of

1977. Though a number of very big fish were caught before the tragedy, it is clear that specimen catches fell off drastically during the following five years. But incredibly, the hardy wrasse made a fantastic recovery and the return of this plucky species is now complete.

The following chart shows a decrease in the number of big wrasse caught after the critical winter of 1963 and a resurgence of good fish in 1969. It also highlights a recent trend in wrasse fishing – the increase in the number of specimens taken from Channel Island waters during winter months. Fish over 5 lb are listed before 1969. Only fish over 6 lb are listed after that year. Details reproduced by courtesy of *Angling Times* files.

Date of capture		Weight	Where caught
1964	August	7 lb 8 oz	Channel Islands
	August	6 lb 3 oz	Channel Islands
1965	November	5 lb 7 oz	Devon
1966	April	6 lb 7 oz	Ireland
	June	7 fish to 5 lb	Devon
	July	6 lb	Channel Islands
	November	7 lb 2 oz	Devon
1967	April	6 lb 2 oz	Cornwall
	October	6 lb 6 oz	Devon
1968	August	5 lb 9½ oz	Cornwall
1969	August	7 lb 2 oz	Cornwall
1970	June	6 lb 3 oz	Devon
	July	6 lb 5¾ oz	Cornwall
	August	6 lb	Devon
	August	6 lb 15 oz	Devon
	August	6 lb 8 oz	Cornwall
	December	7 lb 10 oz 15 dr	Cornwall
1971	October	6 lb	Cornwall

1972	June	6 lb 3 oz	Cornwall
	September	7 over 6 lb	Channel Islands
	September	7 lb 4 oz	Cornwall
	October	6 lb 4 oz	Cornwall
	November	7 lb 2 oz	Channel Islands
1973	August	7 lb 1 oz	Channel Islands
	August	7 lb 8 oz	Cornwall
	August	6 lb 1¾ oz	Devon
	August	6 lb 3 oz 9 dr	Channel Islands
	September	7 lb 6½ oz	Cornwall
	September	6 lb 2 oz	Devon
	October	6 lb 15 oz	Cornwall
	October	6 lb 8 oz 3 dr	Devon
	November	6 lb 7½ oz	Cornwall
1974	January	6 lb 10 oz	Channel Islands
	January	6 lb 8 oz	Devon
	August	6 lb 8 oz	Cornwall
	August	6 lb 9 oz	Channel Islands
	August	6 lb 8 oz	Cornwall
	August	6 lb 4 oz	Cornwall
	August	6 lb 2 oz	Cornwall
	August	7 lb 8 oz	Scilly Isles
	September	6 lb 7 oz	Cornwall
	September	6 lb 4 oz	Cornwall
	September	6 lb 2 oz	Devon
	October	7 lb	Cornwall
	October	6 lb 15 oz	Cornwall
	October	6 lb	Cornwall
	October	7 lb	Cornwall
	October	6 lb 1 oz	Devon
	October	6 lb 10 oz	Cornwall
	October	6 lb 4 oz	Cornwall
	October	6 lb 9 oz	Cornwall
	November	7 lb 4 oz	Channel Islands
	November	6 lb 10 oz	Cornwall
	December	7 lb ¼ oz	Channel Islands
	December	7 lb 3 oz 3 dr	Channel Islands
1975	February	7 lb 9½ oz	Devon
	March	6 lb 11½ oz	Devon

	April	6 lb 13 oz	Channel Islands
	April	6 lb 12¾ oz	Devon
	May	7 lb 6 oz	Cornwall
	May	6 lb 1½ oz	Devon
	June	7 lb 4 oz	Devon
	June	6 lb 12¾ oz	Devon
	July	6 lb 1 oz	Cornwall
	August	6 lb 7¾ oz	Cornwall
	August	7 lb 8 oz 5 dr	Channel Islands (boat record)
	September	7 lb ¾ oz	Cornwall
	September	6 lb 14½ oz	Cornwall
	October	6 lb 2 oz	Devon
	October	7 lb 1 oz	Cornwall
	October	6 lb 7 oz	Cornwall
	October	7 lb 2 oz	Cornwall
	November	7 lb	Devon
	November	6 lb 13 oz	Dorset
	December	6 lb 12 oz	Dorset
1976	February	6 lb 9¾ oz	Devon
	February	6 lb 9¼ oz	Devon
	February	7 lb ½ oz	Channel Islands
	March	6 lb 15½ oz	Channel Islands
	April	7 lb 1 oz	Devon
	April	6 lb 13½ oz	Channel Islands
	June	7 lb ¾ oz	Channel Islands
	June	6 lb 0 oz 2 dr	Channel Islands
	July	8 lb 4 oz	Cornwall
	August	7 lb 1 oz	Cornwall
	August	7 lb 7 oz	Cornwall
	September	7 lb 2 oz	Channel Islands
	September	8 lb 6 oz 6 dr	Channel Islands (shore record)
	November	6 lb 6½ oz	Devon
	December	7 lb 5¼ oz	Devon
	December	6 lb 5 oz	Devon
1977	February	6 lb 1½ oz	Devon

The real resurgence of the wrasse began with the capture of

fish around the 4 lb mark in 1969. An exceptional specimen for that year was the 7 lb 2 oz wrasse landed by P. R. F. Collins and the following summer, Penryn, Cornwall, wrasse specialist Barrie Lawrence set up the then British record with a 7 lb 10 oz 15 dr fish.

Now the number of wrasse in our waters is at a peak. It seems inevitable that the record will soon be broken . . . and a double-figure wrasse is not out of the question. A 12 lb 1 oz wrasse supposedly caught by F. A. Mitchell Hedges in 1912 was thrown off the record list eight years ago when the British Record (rod-caught) Fish Committee decided there was some doubt about the weight of the fish. But fish of this proportion, and bigger specimens, are known to exist.

Not only have double-figure wrasse been hooked and lost by anglers, they have also been seen by skin-divers. Fish well over 10 lb have been seen to leave the cover of their caves and ledges to gulp down huge crabs! These really big wrasse may well be the fish which survived the 1963 freeze-up. And they would probably have grown even bigger if the intensely cold conditions had not also destroyed their diet of crabs and mussels, consequently slowing down the fish's growth rate.

Most wrasse experts agree that wrasse shoal according to sizes with the big ones hunting alone within their own domain. Therefore if you catch a 4 lb fish it is likely that you will catch several more around that size if the fish are in a feeding mood. The bigger specimens are like hermits, living alone in their own crevices and venturing out only to feed. Reports by skin-divers, along with tagging experiments, substantiate this theory. A number of tagging experiments have been carried out to obtain information on the movements of wrasse but rarely has a tagged fish been recaptured more than 100 yards from where it was first caught. In other words wrasse colonise certain areas and big fish will even fight to defend their territory – a perfect illustration of the fish's pugnacious character.

Distribution
The best times for catching wrasse vary in different parts of the country, though it is basically a summer species. Cornwall is

without doubt the prolific area in the country, its coastline and climate being ideally suited to the species. Few other areas of our coastline produce wrasse in any numbers and hardly any are caught off the northern shores.

The Channel Islands, however, have emerged as a big wrasse hotspot over the past two or three seasons and this area in particular has yielded specimens well into the winter months – possibly due to the milder conditions. Generally speaking, May, June, and July are excellent months for catching wrasse, but the state of the tide is a crucial factor. To enjoy maximum sport it is best to begin fishing as the tide makes its way in. Wrasse, like many other species, like to move in with the tide, scouring the rocks for food on their way. The three hours before high water can be relied upon to provide the best results, though it is common to pick up good fish as the tide falls away.

This style of fishing makes it essential to select a mark where you are not going to get cut off by the incoming tide. Skindivers have pointed out that when the tide is low wrasse do not appear to be in a feeding mood and lie dormant some 20 to 25 yards offshore. The presence of plenty of weed – bladder wrack and the long stranded type of kelp – is also very important when picking a spot to fish. Weed may prove a hazard when a fish is hooked and it has provided sanctuary for many wrasse that would otherwise have been landed. But weed also provides cover and protection for the wrasse and harbours the marine life upon which they feed.

Though the wrasse is basically a summer fish, rough conditions do not seem to affect it to any great extent. A gale-force wind was raging when Barrie Lawrence broke the British record and wrasse will feed right through to November if the weather remains reasonably mild.

Early season may be favourite for wrasse fishing but there is no reason why very big fish, even record breakers, should not be caught late in the season. For this is when they are fattening up for the winter, and the same thing applies to the spawning period, usually in July and August. They move out about a mile into the tide rips to make 'nests' from weed and pebbles and during this time they become very deep bellied. The only drawback is that this makes them lethargic and they do not feed so well.

Baits

When it comes to selecting a bait to catch wrasse, crab would certainly get the vote of most anglers, but mussels make up the greatest part of the fish's staple diet. Open the stomach of a wrasse and you will most likely find that mussels make up 80 per cent of its contents, crabs 15 per cent, and miscellaneous food material such as limpets the other five per cent. The fact that wrasse eat so many mussels probably accounts for the effectiveness of crab. A big green crab, conveniently presented by the angler, becomes a delicacy. And the bigger the crab the better because the larger baits tend to sort out the larger fish.

Crabs have several other advantages over other baits. Firstly, they are very easy to use. The hook is simply pushed into the belly at the rear end so that the point protrudes from the top of the crab towards the front. There is little point in impaling the bait a number of times. Hooked only once the crab will stay alive longer and remain on the move, a particular attraction to the hawkeyed wrasse. There is no need to tie it on to the hook with elasticated cotton, a precaution which must be used with other baits such as soft mussel. The angler can fish confidently in the knowledge that his bait is still on the hook. If he does not get a bite in one spot he can reel in to cast elsewhere knowing his bait will still be there.

Though movement is important in a bait it is often a good tactic to cut the bigger crabs in two and use a half at a time. The juice and strong scent released into the water will sometimes make up for the lack of movement. The hard greenback crab is the easiest to use, but the softback and peeler varieties require a different approach. Although the baits are not likely to be thrown off by casting, because only a gentle swing is necessary to lob them into a likely-looking haunt, it is still a good precaution to tie these softer baits on to the hook.

Mussel, another soft bait, will catch plenty of wrasse. So too will ragworm, though this tends to attract the smaller fish in the 2 lb to 3 lb class. Limpet is not so good but it must be remembered that wrasse have voracious appetites and will greedily smash into just about any bait.

Tackle and methods

Whatever the bait, the terminal tackle must be just right to present it in the best way under the conditions prevailing at that time. And most important the tackle must be strong enough to land a fish after it has been hooked. A long rod – not less than 10 feet in length – is essential to get out over the rocky ledges and to control a hooked fish. Anything from a freshwater carp or pike rod to a light beachcaster will do the job provided it will cast 2 oz weights. Rods come in for rough treatment on the rocks. Whippings become frayed and rods can even be cracked so it is important to check them regularly to avoid fish being lost through carelessness.

Multiplier reels are better than fixed-spools, despite the fact that long casting is not necessary. They stand up better to rough treatment and allow far more control when playing a fish. The slipping clutches on most fixed-spool reels just cannot be relied upon when playing a charging wrasse, which could be lost in the weed or rocks if the angler should make one wrong move.

When it comes to line strength the snag-ridden surroundings in which wrasse are caught must be taken into consideration. A line of 18 lb to 20 lb may sound heavy for a species of this size, but anglers who use lighter lines will learn by their mistakes. The first mad rush of a big wrasse has broken heavier lines. And it does not take long for a thick line to fray and break when it is rubbed over sharp rocks and barnacles, especially when there is a wrasse on one end and an angler on the other.

The type of terminal rig used can vary according to conditions. A favourite rig for areas where there is not too much weed but plenty of rock, like the rocky headlands on the north Cornish coast, consists of a leader about 20 feet long and between 20 lb and 30 lb breaking strain. This is tied to the main line with a blood knot. About three feet of 14 lb to 18 lb nylon is then attached to the end of the leader with a swivel and a size 1/0 or 2/0 is tied on the end. Another swivel is allowed to run free on the leader and the weight is attached to this with about one foot of 12 lb nylon (see figure 6).

This rig is similar to a conventional running trace with the 12 lb 'rotten bottom' to help save tackle when the lead becomes snagged in crevices or thick kelp. When pressure is applied to pull out of a snag the 12 lb line breaks first and only the weight is lost. The very nature of wrasse fishing means that many weights are going to be lost in the rocks and it is a costly business for the angler who buys all his weights. Many wrasse anglers get round this problem by using old nuts and bolts or even spark plugs for the job instead of the expensive lead weights on sale in the tackle shops.

More weedy stretches of coastline, like the south coast of Cornwall, demand that another type of rig should be used. This is a simpler affair. No swivels are used and it is not even worth bothering with a leader. About four feet of 12 lb line is attached to the main line so that a two-foot dropper of 18 lb line is also left hanging. The dropper takes the hook and the 12 lb rotten bottom again takes the weight as a safety precaution against lost tackle. The idea of this rig is that while the weight lies buried in the weed the bait lies close to, but just off, the bottom in clear view of any hungry wrasse (see figure 7).

The third method is float fishing. This has produced some very big wrasse and the float is very simple to make and use. Basically the rig comprises a float and a drilled bullet weight big enough to cock it. However, many anglers make the mistake of using the wrong type of float. A slim bodied float which offers little resistance to a taking fish is the answer . . . not a fat, buoyant float which would need a submarine to pull it under!

The main arguments against float fishing are based on bait presentation. As has been explained, wrasse, particularly the very big fish, lie in the most inaccessible of places and you just cannot put a bait in these spots on float gear. Wrasse fishing also demands that the bait be fished hard on the bottom, but you can never be sure at what level the bait is when float fishing. The bottom rises and falls so sharply in wrasse territory that the bait can be lying on a rocky ledge one minute and suspended well off the bottom the next.

FIG 6 Rig for rocky ground with light kelp

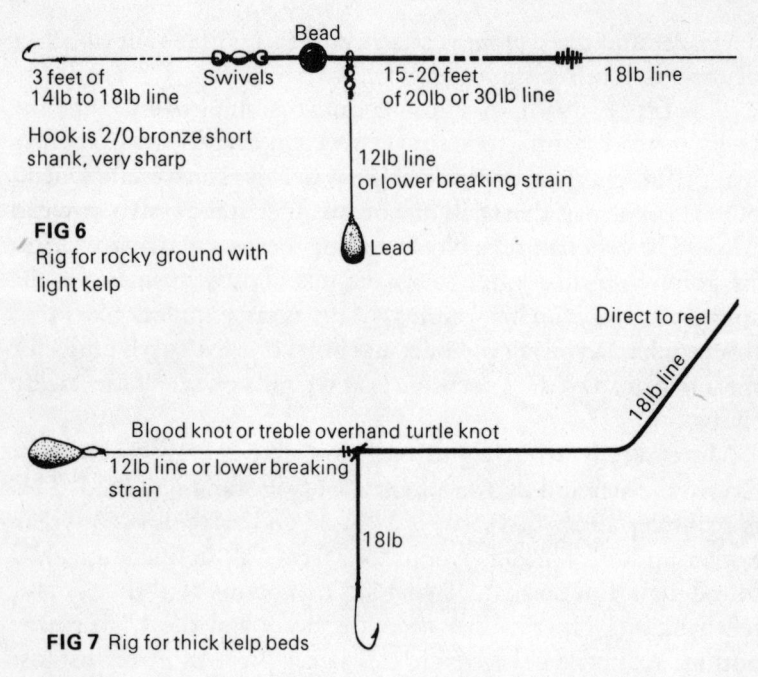

- 3 feet of 14lb to 18lb line
- Swivels
- Bead
- 15-20 feet of 20lb or 30lb line
- 18lb line
- Hook is 2/0 bronze short shank, very sharp
- 12lb line or lower breaking strain
- Lead

FIG 7 Rig for thick kelp beds

- Direct to reel
- 18lb line
- Blood knot or treble overhand turtle knot
- 12lb line or lower breaking strain
- 18lb

Finally we come to, perhaps, the most important part of the tackle, the hook. Choice of hooks is largely a matter of individual preference but most wrasse experts agree that bronze hooks are better than stainless steel. This is because they are finer in body and this gives them better penetration. Wrasse have thick, leathery lips which make it difficult to set a thick-bodied hook. Big hooks, sizes 1/0 and 2/0, are best because they need to carry big baits. Like the rest of the tackle, hooks come in for plenty of rough treatment on the rocks and are easily blunted. Therefore it is essential to sharpen or change them during a day's wrasse fishing.

Wrasse do not give the angler a second chance. Their hit and run tactics mean the angler must hold the rod at all times. Otherwise, he may not only lose the fish but also his rod. More than one angler has seen his rod dragged from the rocks by a charging wrasse. But that's wrasse fishing . . . the thrills and spills make it all worthwhile.

Flounder

This humble species is an obliging fish. Though among the smaller members of the flat-fish family, it is found all around our coast, and is absent only during the spawning period. It penetrates estuaries and often ventures into freshwater. There are many venues where it is likely to be the only species caught from the shore in the winter and it will often provide sport on what would otherwise be a blank outing.

A 2 lb flounder is a good fish, though specimens in the 3 lb class are by no means rare. A flounder over that weight is exceptional, however, and the British boat record – a 5 lb 11½ oz fish taken off Fowey, Cornwall, by A. G. L. Cobbledick – has stood since 1956. The shore record is held by M. King who took a 4 lb 7 oz flounder off Seaford Beach, Sussex, in 1976.

Distribution

Flounders, though available for most of the year under a wide range of conditions, come into their own during the winter. This is partly because the fish is generally in the peak of condition at this time and partly because many other species are not so easily caught. The fish are ready for spawning, which takes place from January to April depending on the area. This, therefore, is an ideal time for the big fish man. The roes and livers will be large, adding valuable extra weight.

Flounders move several miles offshore to spawn and as a result are rarely caught on rod and line during this period. After spawning they return to their inshore feeding grounds and the estuaries. They are in poor condition at this time but feed heavily and quickly recover.

Tackle and methods

One of the greatest attractions of the flounder is that it is relatively easy to catch. Ultra-light tackle is by no means essential and they are often caught on tackle intended for other species such as cod. But by adopting the right approach, you can enjoy an exciting day's fishing with flounders instead of catching just the occasional fish. Fortunately, catching flounders doesn't mean sticking rigidly to one particular method. They can be caught from the beach, boat, and pier and will take a legered, float fished, or spun bait.

Legering is the most effective, and therefore, most popular method. A simple home-made paternoster with two six-inch snoods spaced about 18 inches apart is ideal (see figure 8). This rig keeps both baits clear of the lead and provides plenty of

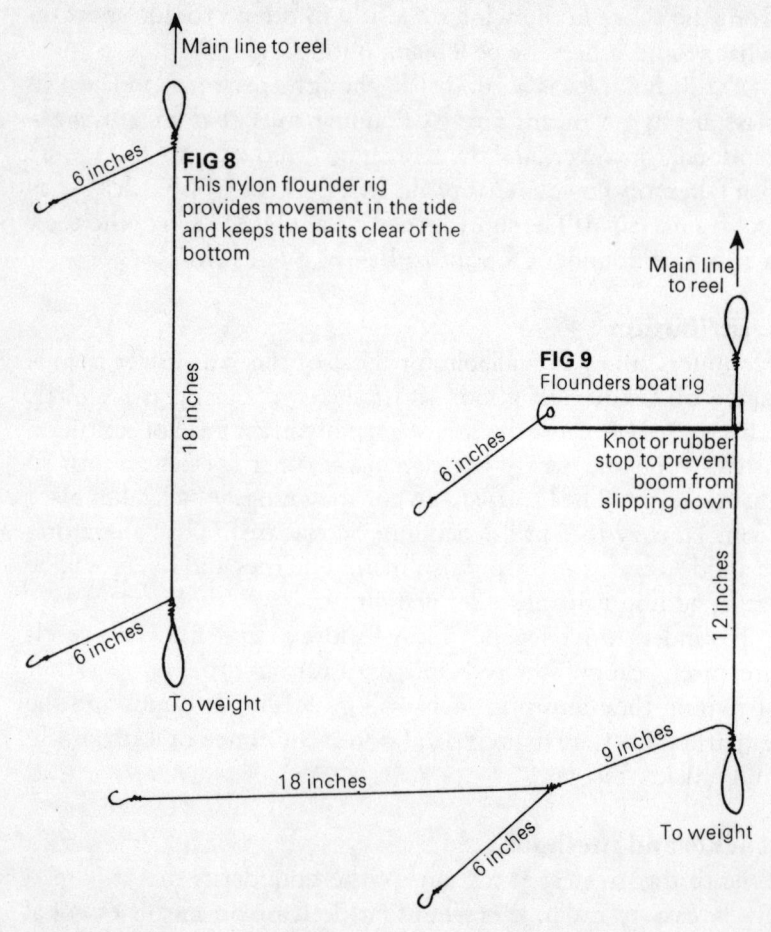

FIG 8
This nylon flounder rig provides movement in the tide and keeps the baits clear of the bottom

FIG 9
Flounders boat rig

Knot or rubber stop to prevent boom from slipping down

48

attractive movement in the tide. The weight itself should be as light as possible, though this does, of course, depend on the strength of the tide. Remember also that the weight must be heavy enough to allow a good long cast if necessary. Balance the weight correctly with the tide and the strength of the current will move the rig across the sea bed in an arc, covering a far greater area than would be possible if the tackle was anchored to the bottom with a hefty weight. Movement of the tackle can be encouraged by allowing a little slack in the line.

When fishing from the shore for flounders the best sport is generally just before high water. They have a tendency to move into deep water or into the shelter of gullies when the tide ebbs and this is an important point for the boat angler to remember.

Flounders are not a timid fish when it comes to taking a bait and they are most confident when the water is a little coloured. Often there will be no preliminary messing about with the bait to warn the angler a fish is, at least, interested. The fish will take the angler's offering wholeheartedly, registering a very definite knock on the rod top. The power of a flounder is deceiving. It may appear as a fragile species, but its relatively long tail makes it a powerful swimmer and it will invariably give a good account of itself on the right tackle. A light beachcaster and a line of say 12 lb, to cope with any snags or bigger species that may put in an unexpected appearance, is quite strong enough.

It is easy to be misled when choosing a hook for flounder fishing. For though the fish does not have a big mouth it can be a mistake to use a hook that is too small. Admittedly a small hook is easy for the fish to take into its mouth, but it is equally easy for it to eject it again. A 1/0 hook is ideal. Even small flounders will have no difficulty in sucking it into their mouths.

Spoon fishing is a popular and sporting method of catching flounders and can be carried out from both the shore and boats. Anglers using spoons from the shore should never be too intent on casting long distances but should pay attention to the water close in. Casting parallel to the shore and working the spoon back through shallow water will often produce far more fish. A big spoon will not deter even the smallest flounders from moving in to attack and the effectiveness of the lure is improved when it is baited with a piece of worm.

Many anglers, however, prefer to fish spoons from a boat, either spinning them or trolling them behind the boat. Both methods take fish and so too does a third style of spoon fishing. The lure is suspended clear of the bottom on a sliding float. The greatest advantage of this method being that it is possible to cover a large area by allowing the float to move with the tide. The bait is also less likely to be interfered with by greedy crabs which always seem to abound on flounder marks.

Another good method of tackling flounders from a boat, probably the most effective of all, is a variation on the legering theme (see figure 9). A conventional two-hook trace is used just above the weight, one hook on a short length of line, say six inches, and the other on a longer length, perhaps as long as 18 inches. But in addition another hook is used on a white, flat plastic or nylon boom further up the main line. A slight kink or twist in the boom will make it move in the tide and attract flounders or other flatties to the three baits on offer. It is by no means a rarity to catch two or even three fish at the same time on a multi-hook rig such as this.

This method of boat fishing works best when the tide is not too strong. For when this is the case only an ounce to one and a half ounces of lead are needed on a light rod and the angler can cover quite a wide area by casting with or across the tide. Remember that the greatest advantage of boat fishing is that it allows you to search out the deeper gullies and creeks which cannot be fished from the shore.

Baits
When it comes to baits the flounder has eyes bigger than its belly. It has been caught on just about every accepted bait, and a few more besides, at one time or another. The best all-round bait, however, is ragworm. Size is not that important but when a big worm is used it often pays to give the fish a little extra time to get it well into its mouth before striking.

Ragworm are at their most effective during the early part of the winter. After spawning flounders will gleefully mop up lugworms, crabs, mussels, small strips of fish, and they have even taken earthworms. This is not so surprising when you consider flounders penetrate well up our rivers where earthworms are naturally available.

As a rule flounders tend to move inshore late on the tide and their peak period of feeding activity is at dusk. So if you time your fishing to coincide with dusk and a late tide, you could be in for a big supper.

Soles

These are not the most popular species in the flat-fish family, basically because they are rarer than most and because they do not grow as big as turbot, flounder, plaice, and brill. The British record stands at 4 lb 3½ oz (shore-caught) while the record for the lemon sole, which is not so widespread, is held by a 2 lb 2 oz specimen.

Distribution
Though not as common as other flat-fish, the sole is not a rarity. Few anglers specialise in them and many of those taken are caught by accident. But the angler looking particularly for soles can catch them quite frequently, especially in hotspots like the Kent and Sussex coasts. The best time is from June until the end of August. You will not see them during the winter, when they move out into deeper water with most other summer species. The best opportunities for catching soles come at dusk, for, although they are a summer species, you will not catch many when the sun is blazing down. Low water at dusk is ideal and it is quite possible to take as many as a dozen soles during the two hours just before and just after low tide. An hour's fishing either side of high water can also be productive, particularly if the sea is well coloured after a strong wind.

Tackle and methods
One of the greatest attractions of catching soles is that you do not have to hurl your tackle long distances to find the fish. Choose a nice sandy beach and you can catch them 20 yards out and perhaps even closer on occasions. When it comes to terminal tackle, simplicity is the key. A small hook is essential. Soles do not have very large mouths and a size 6/0 will do the job nicely. A straightforward running trace about two and a half feet long is ideal and you don't have to limit yourself to one hook. Three

hooks, each baited with tiny pieces of lugworm or ragworm, will increase your chances.

It is by no means unlikely that this rig will account for more than one fish on the same cast. Soles move in shoals. Catch one and you can bet there are more of them around, so don't waste time. Put another bait on quickly and try to drop it into the same spot.

Hooking a sole is slightly more difficult than getting it to take the bait. Don't worry about the bite. The sole is a powerful little fish and will register a sharp jerk after first revealing its presence via a slight knock on the rod top. But it pays to wait a few seconds after the first sign of a bite to make sure the fish has time to suck the bait into its mouth. The fish will leave you in no doubt as to when to pull it in.

You won't go home with aching arms after a good session catching soles, but you will have some enjoyment. Sole fishing is fun and there is no need to fish at night. And they taste delicious!

Dabs

Some anglers claim that dabs were created as small fish so that they would fit into a frying pan, for eaten fresh they are among the tastiest fish in the sea. But because they lack weight – dabs over 1 lb 8 oz are rarely caught on rod and line – they do not attract as much attention from the angling fraternity as the bigger varieties of flat-fish. They are often caught for the pot rather than the sport.

Distribution
Nevertheless, the diminutive dab can provide a lot of fun if approached in the correct way and with light tackle. There is certainly no shortage of them around the British Isles for they have been caught just about everywhere at one time or another. They are probably most thickly distributed around the south-east corner of England and along the south coast. But they are also caught in numbers as far north as Shetland where Lerwick Harbour has developed into a dab hotspot in recent years. They have also been caught by English anglers on trips to Iceland!

Dabs favour sandy, muddy ground with the bigger specimens being found mainly on the sand banks favoured by turbot and brill. An angler catching dabs will take it as a sign that turbot are likely to be in the area and vice versa. After spawning offshore dabs will move on to the inshore grounds from about May onwards. Some will venture very close to the shore, feeding freely both in daylight and darkness. They begin to move out again into deeper water at the onset of winter, though sometimes their movements will follow the coastline and they will enter estuaries and harbours for short periods.

This means that dabs are not necessarily purely a summer species from the angler's point of view. Indeed, some excellent catches are made during December and January and many anglers regard this as the peak period. The time of year does, of course, depend on the area being fished and generally speaking the offshore sand banks which tend to produce the biggest dabs fish best during the warmer months. All fish are unpredictable, however, and the dab is no exception.

Find a sandy bottom and dabs will not be far away. That is the main rule to remember when searching out these tasty flatties. It also pays to remember that dabs will be close to mussel beds, for they love to feed on the tiny mussels which measure only about three-eighths of an inch across. The dab has a varied diet, details of which will be found overleaf.

Tackle and methods
Boats offer more scope when dab fishing, allowing you to explore more grounds and deeper water than could be reached from the beach. Dabs are influenced by the temperature of the water and when it is cold they will often move into the warmer, deeper water. Boat fishing means there is no danger of breaking your line when casting a weight, because the tackle is just lowered over the side. Therefore it is possible to scale down to a very light line, say 10 lb, and a soft-action, hollow glass-fibre rod of about eight feet to get the very best from the dabs.

Simplicity is the key when it comes to deciding on the choice of terminal tackle. A three-foot running trace carrying three small hooks on short nylon snoods fits the bill perfectly.

Beach fishing is a slightly different proposition. In this case the three hooks should be presented above the weight. Dabs will very often take a bait just off the bottom rather than one fished hard on the sea bed. It is also an advantage to use the action of the tide to provide some sort of movement to the rig. The weight should be of the grip lead variety so that the angler can shorten the gripping wires, allowing the rig to move slowly along with the tide. As with most fish, movement and sound arouse the dab's curiosity.

The importance of the distance achieved in the cast from the beach depends on wind conditions. Dabs tend to move in closer when there is an onshore wind, and move further out when the wind is offshore. Unfortunately, tackle cannot be so light when fishing from the shore. A beachcaster of about 11 feet 6 inches in length must be used to achieve long-distance casting and the line must be at least 15 lb breaking strain to withstand the continual casting of a hefty weight.

Baits
As stated earlier, the natural diet of dabs includes quite a variety of food organisms. Michael Kennedy in his book *The Sea Angler's Fishes* states that 'the diet of the dab varies according to the locality – depending on the kind of food organisms most abundant'. Dabs taken from the Firth of Forth and St Andrew's Bay in Scotland and from the Irish Sea were found to contain razor fish, crabs, sand stars, other bivalves and flesh from sand-eels, young herrings, and lugworms and other sand worms. So it appears that the dab is not fussy when it comes to meals. From the angling point of view, however, small strips of fish have emerged as the best baits, especially for the bigger fish. Herring and mackerel are the most widely used baits for rod and line caught dabs.

But as that mixed diet suggests, dabs can be taken on a number of other baits, including small pieces of lugworm, ragworm, and even garden worms. The garden worm is capable of tempting other species such as plaice, flounders, and cod as well as dabs. The best worms to use are those off-white, hard little worms measuring anything from about one and a half to three inches in length. Use them whole on the hook.

Anyone who decides to specialise in dab fishing should set their target at 2 lb 12¼ oz, the British boat-caught record set up by R. Islip in Scotland's Gairloch in 1975; or 2 lb 9½ oz, the shore-caught record established by M. Watts at Port Talbot, Wales, way back in 1936.

Mackerel

It is a hard but sad fact that the mackerel is regarded solely as bait for other fish by the vast majority of anglers. For though it is true that more fish are caught on mackerel baits of various forms than any other single bait, these fish are one of a number of the smaller class of sea fish which can provide good sport in their own right. The mackerel's problem has always been its size. The best one ever taken on rod and line weighed 5 lb 6½ oz when caught by S. Beasley over the Eddystone mark off Plymouth, Devon, in 1969. And though it has been recorded to over 7 lb in the nets of commercial fishermen, rod and line caught mackerel normally run from 1 lb to 2 lb. A 3 lb mackerel is an excellent fish by anglers' standards.

In appearance the mackerel has been compared to a torpedo because of its round streamlined body which tapers away to nose and tail. As with most fish the distinctive colouring is on the back where it is normally a greenish blue. Wavy black bands run across the back along the length of the body and disappear into the grey flanks and silver belly of the fish.

Mackerel feed on plankton during spring and early summer before spawning, but at other times they vary this plankton diet with fish fry such as herring, pilchard, and sprats, as well as sand-eels. They will also eat the occasional shellfish, such as shrimps, during the summer.

Distribution
The mackerel is its own worst enemy in that it is a very obliging fish and it is not far from the truth to say that any fool can catch it. In addition these 'kami-kaze' fish are widely distributed throughout British waters and are caught both inshore and offshore – from rocks, piers, harbour walls, and boats – by a large number of methods. They are caught all around the British Isles and it is significant that the National Angling Survey published

by the National Anglers' Council, reveals mackerel to be among the most frequently caught species inhabiting our shores.

The mackerel cannot be categorised as a bottom or surface feeding fish. Vast numbers of fish collect in large shoals which roam the sea at various depths, though usually they favour the middle and surface areas of water. It is no wonder then that the mackerel is regarded primarily as a bait fish as it is easy to obtain, free of charge, and very effective. Even freshwater anglers buy them in large numbers from fishmongers during the pike fishing season.

Mackerel are summer fish, arriving inshore by the middle of June at the earliest and moving out into their deep-water winter haunts by October. This, coupled with the fact that they are easy to catch, makes them a favourite fish with holidaymakers who fish the sea only once or twice a year. These holiday anglers find that mackerel will venture surprisingly close inshore in the harbours and along the beaches as they hungrily follow the movements of small fry.

Tackle and methods

When mackerel are in a feeding mood they will take just about any offering in blind ignorance. The subtle approach required to catch mullet is not needed here. The easiest method of catching them in numbers – it is also the most unsporting – is by feathering (see figure 10). A string of feathered hooks is tied to the reel line and a small weight is attached at the other end. The technique of feathering is as simple as the make-up of the rig. The feathers are lowered over the side to a certain depth – depending on the depth at which the mackerel are feeding – and are then moved up and down in the water by the angler raising and lowering his rod. Unless they reveal themselves by feeding on the surface, the whereabouts of mackerel can only be discovered by trial and error. Vary the depth of the feathers until you locate them.

There is no necessity to watch for bites or to strike into the fish. Mackerel simply grab the brightly coloured feathers as they flutter on the hook and hook themselves. There is no skill attached and mackerel can be caught six at a time by this method,

← 6 inches →

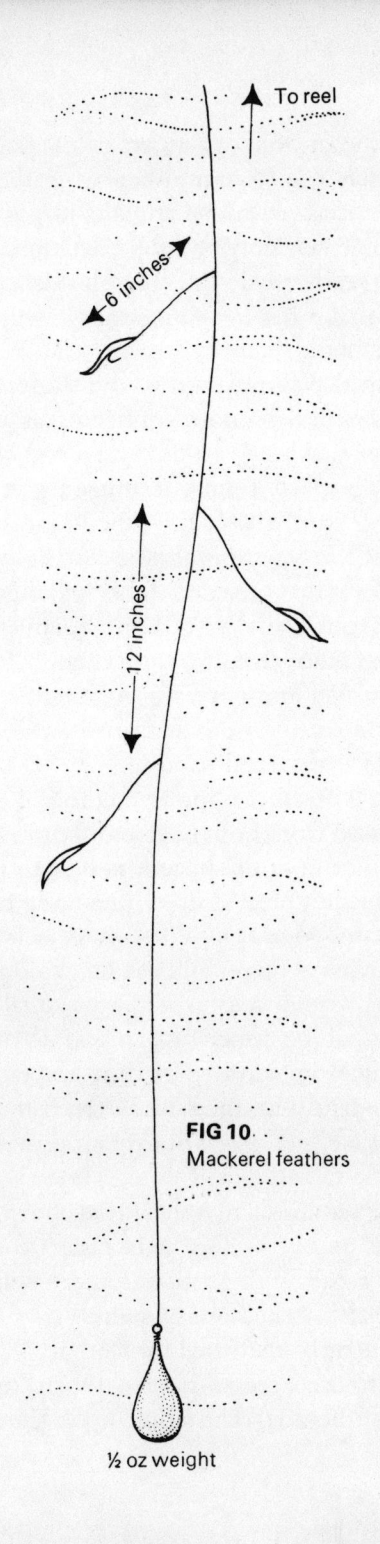

← 12 inches →

FIG 10
Mackerel feathers

½ oz weight

To reel

depending on the amount of feathers on the trace. Unfortunately too many anglers use large numbers of feathers and needlessly butcher far too many fish. Most clubs impose a 'three-feather' rule which should certainly be adopted nationally. Feather traces can be bought ready made-up, though it is a simple matter for the angler to make his own by simply whipping a hackle of feathers on the hook shank.

Feathering is also popular from the shore, particularly with holidaymakers who do not go sea fishing as a rule and employ their freshwater tackle. A 10-foot carp rod, a fixed-spool reel loaded with 8 lb to 10 lb line, terminating in a feather trace is ideal for casting from the rocks. The line could be lighter but for the fact that the weight is almost certain to become snagged in weed or rocks at one time or another and the extra line strength will be needed to free it. The fighting qualities of mackerel will surprise anyone who has not caught them before. They are tremendously fast fish and powerful for their size. One mackerel provides a good scrap on the described tackle and two or three on the same trace are a real handful.

Float fishing is another popular method of catching mackerel which can be used from both boat and shore. When fishing deep water from either boat or shore it is best to use a sliding float rig. Trying to fish 30 feet deep with a fixed float will certainly provide problems! Many anglers seem to believe that float fishing in the sea requires huge, bulbous floats. On the contrary, the float should be as small as possible. A small, slim pike float carrying about half an ounce of lead will do nicely.

When fishing from a boat just drop the tackle over the side and allow it to drift with the tide. When fishing from the shore a cast is, of course, necessary but much ground can be covered by allowing the float to drift along. Locating the fish with a sliding float rig remains a matter of trial and error. When mackerel are visible on the surface it is easier to use a fixed float. Mackerel take a bait with gusto and there will be no mistaking a bite as the float is jerked out of sight.

Tackle is similar to that used for feathering, except that some anglers prefer to use a centre-pin reel for trotting their floats out with the run of the tide. The single hook should be size 4 or 6.

Small fresh slices of fish, especially mackerel, are good baits, along with sand-eel and whitebait. Artificial baits will also be readily taken and spinning from a small boat is one of the most deadly methods. The choice of lures is wide. Anything flashy or brightly coloured will soon attract mackerel and the lure can be a spinner or a spoon which wobbles rather than spins when retrieved. The lure need not be longer than one and a half inches. Since the possibility of getting snagged is minimal, the line can be scaled down to about 7 lb for spinning and the rod should be the conventional eight feet for a spinning rod. Spinning is probably the most sporting and enjoyable way of catching mackerel.

When boat fishing, a shoal of mackerel will often reveal its presence as the fish break surface while chasing fry. Mackerel feeding on the surface a good distance away are sometimes given away by the flocks of gulls feeding on the same fry.

Mackerel are as scarce in winter as they are abundant in summer. By October the mackerel season has ended for the angler. But it is just beginning for the commercial fisherman. The mackerel fishing industry on the south Cornish coast is one of the biggest in Britain and the catches taken by the boats are so massive that the future of the mackerel is being threatened.

The shoals of winter mackerel which gather from along the south coast into the curve of coastline between the Eddystone Reef and Lizard Point have long supported a fishing fleet of some 300 small boats. But a new feature appeared at the beginning of the 1974 season – big trawlers.

The effect of the giant scoops of fish that are not given the chance to spawn can already be seen. The shoals are more scattered, returns of fish are well down, and poor catches are becoming more frequent. And the fact that the pressure on mackerel shoals is bound to increase is bad news for the angler – and for one of our most important sea fish.

Plaice

This is the most popular of the smaller range of flat-fish. Its distribution is fairly widespread, and it is relatively easy to catch, growing to a size which makes the plaice a sporting proposition on the right kind of tackle. Though more prolific in the warmer water off our southern coastline, it is also caught farther north, and the boat record is presently held with a 10 lb 3½ oz fish taken off the west coast of Scotland. The shore record came from Southend Pier in 1976. It weighed 8 lb 1¼ oz and was caught by N. Mills.

Distribution

The boat record was caught in November, 1974, but this plaice was very much an exception to the rule. For plaice are without doubt a summer species. A scorching hot day, a flat calm and clear water over a sandy bottom are ideal plaice fishing conditions. The hotter the summer the more plaice you are likely to catch. The milder the winter the sooner you will begin catching them. Plaice fishing generally gets off the ground in May and fades off towards the end of September, depending on the temperature. As a rule these handsome fish favour shallow water over sandy ground. The Shambles Bank off Weymouth, the Skerries Bank off Dartmouth, and the Varne Bank off Folkestone are all top plaice-fishing marks off the south coast.

The bigger fish, however, while still showing a preference for sandy ground, often tend to hug closest to the rocks. Therefore, it is a good idea to fish sandy patches surrounded by rock. This type of ground has an added advantage in that trawlers dare not operate in the vicinity of rocks for fear of losing their nets. Such spots are not easily found and it is wise to study an Admiralty chart of the area before trying to locate one. Then by using an echo sounder to find it, take careful bearings on the shoreline so that you know the exact location. Inshore rocky areas are well marked on the charts and it is a simple matter to 'feel' your way on to the sand. It is easy to tell what sort of ground you are fishing over by the way the weight bounces on the bottom.

Time taken finding the right mark is well spent. Unless you know a particular spot has produced plaice before, it is often a case of trial and error . . . an hour's fishing here and an hour there until you find the fish. But once your bait is taken by one plaice you can be sure there will be more close by.

Tackle and methods

Plaice can be caught from the shore, but this is not nearly as productive as boat fishing. Most plaice experts favour fishing the shallow inshore marks from small boats, for a number of reasons, mainly because the deeper offshore marks are the targets of commercial fishermen and it does not take long for a trawl net to clear out a productive plaice mark. The shallow water further in makes it impossible for the trawler to operate.

There is also a plentiful supply of mussels inshore. Mussels – the shellfish that form the staple diet of the plaice – attach themselves to inshore rocks and provide huge feeding grounds which can stretch for miles parallel to the shoreline. These grounds cannot be reached by even the best shorecaster so a boat is essential. Bigger mussel beds are found two to three miles offshore in up to 14 fathoms of water. These beds can often be fishing well and then suddenly one day sport will come to an end. This is not because the plaice move, but because the mussels, like other sorts of shellfish, are mobile, and if conditions do not suit them in one area they will move to another. The plaice will duly follow.

Finding the fish again may mean experimenting but there are certain signs to look for which help reveal the whereabouts of plaice. If you are not sure whether the plaice have yet moved inshore, keep a watch out for mackerel moving on the surface. If the mackerel are in, then so are the plaice. Starfish are also a good sign. These delightful creatures also feed on mussels and if you start to reel them up you can bet that plaice are in the area. Also keep an eye open for small rocks with clusters of mussels clinging to them. These can also betray the presence of plaice.

The diet of the plaice is not made up entirely of mussels, however. They are also very partial to another type of shellfish which measures only about an eighth of an inch in length and resembles a miniature whelk. At least this is the case off the south coast where it is quite common to catch plaice stuffed full of them, particularly in areas where there is a muddy bottom.

Since plaice are best caught from a boat, the angler is then faced with the question of whether to fish at anchor or on the drift. In some instances he has no choice. Anglers fishing off the Kent coast, for example, cannot afford to drift because they would lose tremendous amounts of terminal tackle in the rocks. But the famous Skerries mark, off Dartmouth in Devon, is a different proposition. The ground here is undulating but tackle is less likely to get snagged. A good way of covering different ground when fishing at anchor is to let out increasing lengths of anchor cable at about 20 feet a time. This is also a good way to search out the sandy pockets between the rocks. Alternatively you can change the position of the boat by tying the rudder over one way or the other so the tide pushes the boat in different directions.

Terminal tackle is varied to suit conditions, but the most popular rig is a conventional three-hook flowing trace (see figure 11). This is about three feet long and the two upper hooks are attached via six-inch snoods. Size 2/0 hooks are fine. Plaice are greedy fish and gulp the bait positively. A hook of this size should have no trouble finding a secure hold. This simple rig is excellent when used in areas where there are few snags, but it can cause problems when there are rocks in the vicinity. In this case a two-hook spreader with booms six to eight inches long does the job more efficiently.

The main advantage of this compact rig is that the short, stiff booms are less likely to get snagged than the flowing trace, which will be moved around by the tide. Secondly, the plaice can spot the baits from whichever direction they approach the rig. But when a flowing trace is used all three baits are carried downtide.

Movement of the bait is essential. Plaice are curious, like most other fish, and the movement will serve as an added attraction.

Danish angler Hans Christian Clausen caught this 15 lb 10 oz turbot on mackerel strip off Plymouth, Devon. The fish was caught during the European Federation Festival and won the heaviest flatfish prize.

Plymouth angler Ray Dower with a specimen spotted ray taken while boat fishing in local waters.

Young Tim Raymond, of New Romney, Kent, with a 33 lb 2 oz cod which he caught while fishing from Dungeness beach.

A good cod makes a final bid for freedom as it nears the waiting gaff. Captor Dave Petty was fishing off Portsmouth, Hampshire.

Dave Petty was well pleased with this 20 lb cod, caught over the Spoils Ground off Portsmouth, Hampshire.

Piers are always a popular choice for anglers fishing in competitions. This picture shows a crowded North Pier at Seaham, County Durham, during the 1978 International Shore Championships.

Mike Chapman, of Tonbridge, Kent, caught this 9½ lb bass while fishing from the shore at Dungeness.

John Trust, co-skipper of Britain's best known wrecking boat – 'Our Unity' out of Brixham, Devon – brings a dour struggle to its end as he gaffs a good conger.

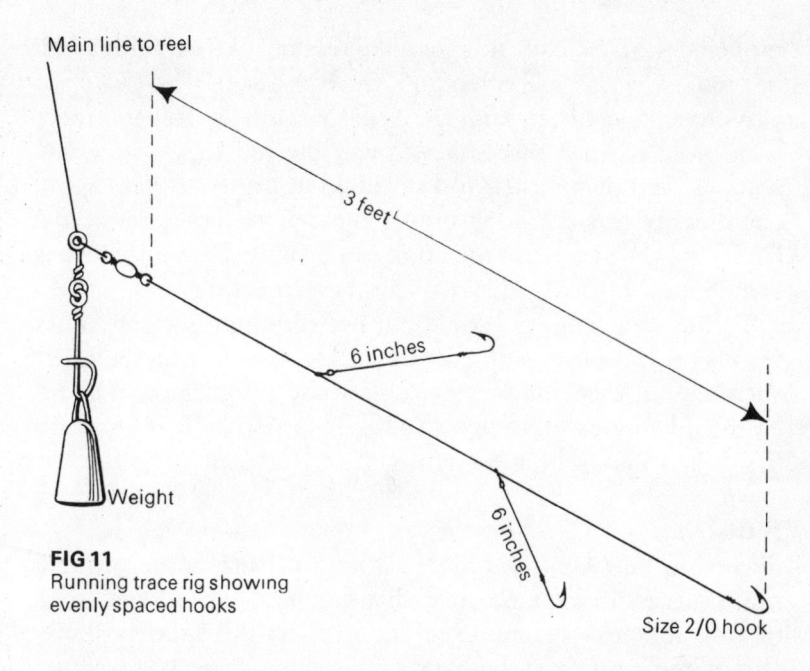

FIG 11
Running trace rig showing evenly spaced hooks

Some experts adopt the 'bouncing' tactic. They drop their weight down to the sea bed and then bounce it slowly on the bottom before lowering the rod top sharply to provide a little slack line. This slack is important because, if a plaice feels resistance when taking the bait, he will very quickly blow it out of his mouth again. For this same reason it is a good idea to drop the rod top at the first sign of a bite, giving the fish time to get the bait well into its mouth. Give a plaice enough rope to hang itself and it will do just that.

A slightly heavier weight than is necessary is advantageous when 'bouncing' for plaice. It not only helps in the actual process, but also prevents the bait being pushed downtide if there is a strong run. It is also probable that the plaice hear the bump of the weight on the bottom and move in for a closer look. When plaice are very finicky, a more subtle version of bouncing can be adopted to tempt them to take a bait. Keeping a tight line, slowly raise the rod a few inches. This slight movement is transmitted right down the line to the trace and causes a slight movement of the bait. It is just like teasing a kitten with a ball of wool. The fish will often gulp the bait down.

As has already been said, the plaice is a greedy fish and there is no need to rush the strike. Lower the rod top, wait a few seconds, and then lift the rod steadily but firmly. A hard strike could easily tear the hook out of the delicate tissue inside the fish's mouth. Similarly, the hook can be pulled out if the fish is swung into the boat, so it is always best to net them.

Tackle-wise, anglers should not use very light rods and lines for plaice. It is only asking for the tackle to be lost on the rocks surrounding their sandy lairs. Use a line and a trace of about 25 lb and snoods of 10 lb to 15 lb. The snoods then break off first when a hook becomes snagged.

Baits

Plaice can be taken on a wide variety of baits, some proving more successful in some areas than others. Sand-eel and strips of fish, for instance, are excellent baits on the Skerries Bank. But off the Kent coast, on marks such as the Varne, a tiny sliver of mackerel tipped with a small piece of lugworm is the top bait. An ideal sliver is two inches long and three-eighths of an inch across, preferably cut from across the full width of the mackerel.

Finally, remember that plaice will normally feed when the tide is moving, for fish generally take the opportunity of resting during slack water.

Haddock

The haddock is closely related to the cod and resembles it in appearance. It is smaller in size than the cod, however, and can be easily identified by its forked tail and distinctive dark patch on each shoulder. Like the cod it has a barbule or 'beard' below the lower jaw. In most areas where it is commonly caught, haddock averages 3 lb to 4 lb. The present British boat record stands at 12 lb 10 oz 1 dr, but more about that fish and the circumstances of its capture later.

Sadly, haddock have suffered greatly from the pressures of commercial fishing. The soft sandy or muddy grounds over which they are found are easy picking for the trawlers. With no rocks to protect them from the nets, haddock have been seriously depleted over the years – particularly in the North Sea where they were once extremely thick on the ground.

Haddock are bottom feeders and have a tremendously varied diet. They are particularly fond of crustaceans, mainly shrimps and crabs, plus razorfish, whelks, worms, and squid. They will also take herring and sprats on occasions though they are not prolific fish eaters. They take up residence close inshore from November to February but move offshore to spawn during the summer.

Haddock are a shoal fish caught from boats. They do not venture close enough inshore to make them a sporting proposition for anglers fishing from pier, beach, or rocks. The present shore record of 6 lb 12 oz, taken from Scotland's Loch Goil in 1976 by G. Stevenson, was the exception rather than the rule. They are not a particularly hard fighting species but they are a popular table fish, especially smoked. The NFSA specimen weight for haddock is 4 lb.

From the angling viewpoint there are only three areas around our coasts where haddock fishing is really worthwhile – Cornwall, Yorkshire, and the west of Scotland.

CORNWALL

The 'county of pasties' has emerged as good haddock fishing territory only in recent years. It was crowned the undisputed 'king' of haddock country in January 1975 when Sub-Lieutenant Ken White of the Naval Air Station at Culdrose boated his staggering 12 lb 10 oz 1 dr British record specimen off the well-known Manacles mark. That fish had a tremendous impact on the angling world, and not just because of its size, for the record had seemed to be resting firmly in the hands of a certain Joe Hill who had captured a 10 lb 12 oz haddock – a sensational catch at the time – off Looe, Cornwall, in 1972. Then came the sequence of events leading to the capture of Ken White's fish.

Ironically, the fish came from a mark discovered almost by accident. Ken, skipper of a naval launch which took Culdrose Angling Club members out from Falmouth, had cod in mind when he located a mark reputedly good for this species. But that first trip, in December, produced a 5 lb 13½ oz haddock for club member Mick Oliver . . . and no cod! Two return trips to the same mark confirmed that here was a haddock ground supreme. For Mick Oliver took two more fish of 7 lb 15 oz and 7 lb 5 oz. The hunt was on for the British record fish they knew must be there. Bob Bell shaved the target with a 10 lb 3¼ oz fish and on another trip a dozen haddock, including six over 4 lb, were pulled from the 30 fathom mark, less than a mile from the Manacles. Many more were lost.

Lugworm was the killing bait, though mackerel strip and squid had produced fish. A bunch of worms on a 3/0 hook produced cautious bites which had to be given time before striking. The haddock also had to be boated carefully, preferably with a net, or the hooks would tear out of their soft mouths.

So by the time Sunday 26 January – record breaking day – came, Ken knew all about the big Cornish haddock. The bite from the record fish followed the usual pattern and Ken played the fish carefully for 20 minutes before boating it. Ironically it was only the second fish Ken had caught during the haddock onslaught. His first one weighed only 2 lb. The fun did not end with Ken's record fish. Mick Oliver took an 11 lb 8 oz specimen a week later. And all the anglers who fished the productive mark are convinced much bigger fish are there to be caught. A haddock of more than 20 lb has reputedly been taken from Irish waters and there are records of numerous other fish over the British record being caught in nets.

YORKSHIRE

The Yorkshire coast once held the haddock record, even if it was only for 48 hours. The 9 lb-plus specimen was quickly overtaken by a West Country fish, but it is an indication of the size of haddock that can be caught in the area. After cod, they are probably the most heavily distributed species off the Yorkshire coast. Yorkshire haddock tend to run in two 'grades'. First there are the jumbo haddock – fish of 4 lb to 5 lb and upwards which gather in big shoals. These are the fish which interest the rod and line angler. But then there are the fish known to local anglers as 'fish-shop' haddock which average about 10 inches in length. These are the fish which interest the commercial fishermen.

If an angling boat runs across a concentration of these fish-shop haddock it will move on in search of bigger haddock or perhaps cod. But when jumbo haddock start to turn up the boat will stay put and search out the mark. Many anglers wrongly believe that there is little difference between haddock and cod fishing. There is, in fact, a distinct difference in the types of ground favoured by these fish off the Yorkshire coast. Cod prefer rocky scaurs and kelp beds while haddock frequent soft, sandy ground. The major problem here is that this type of ground is very vulnerable to fishing by trawlers, which can operate without fear of losing or tearing their nets on rocks. For this reason local anglers who know the whereabouts of the best haddock grounds never reveal them, thus limiting the activities of the trawlermen to a minimum.

Yorkshire anglers have a word for good haddock ground. They call it the 'soft'. These areas of 'soft' are normally found only about a mile offshore and the fact that you do not need a big boat to reach them is one of the attractions of fishing them. A 10-foot dinghy and a 5 h.p. engine will do the job nicely, providing weather conditions are absolutely dependable.

Tackle and methods
Baits are numerous. Mussel and worm are the most conventional, but prawns, shrimps, and sand-eel will all catch fish. Some anglers use frozen sand-eel to particularly good effect, collecting them on the beaches with shrimp nets and immediately freezing them down for use in the future. Shrimp is a good bait but, because it is so soft, it is essential to hook the fish on the first knock. Sand-eel, being tougher, are more difficult to get off the hook.

Haddock can be caught both at anchor or by drifting. If a shoal of haddock is on the move it is possible to follow the shoal on the drift. But if the fish appear to be milling around and feeding on the same area of sea bed it is possible to drop the anchor and fish directly over them.

A simple paternoster is the favourite terminal tackle with Yorkshire anglers. The normal procedure is to begin fishing with the weight hard on the bottom. If that does not produce fish the next step is to take in a few turns of line to see if results are better just off the bottom. This trial and error type fishing is continued until the haddock are located. Remember to count the turns of the reel when lifting the tackle off the bottom so that the bait can be returned to that depth if it should prove successful. For where there is one haddock there are sure to be more. Float fishing can also prove effective for haddock off the Yorkshire coast. A sliding float rig can be dropped over the side and the bait drifted downtide to the fish.

Lines used in this part of the country are usually the same for haddock as for cod – about 35 lb. For the usual approach is to try for haddock on the inshore grounds and to move further out on to the cod grounds if haddock fail to show. But for the real haddock specialist, a line of 15 lb would be better. There are few snags to worry about on the 'soft' and a finer line would bring better results and greater sport with hooked fish.

The truth is, however, that anglers in this area are not specimen minded. They are primarily interested in quantity, not quality, and the boat skippers are most concerned with finding plenty of fish for their customers. There are so few people actually looking for big haddock that the true potential for this species has never been realised.

As mentioned earlier, the west coast of Scotland is also good haddock territory. The lochs and the waters surrounding the islands are densely populated with haddock, though these fish are rather smaller than those caught on other parts of the coast. A straightforward paternoster is all that is required in the way of terminal tackle. They are also taken on the heavy pirks popular for cod fishing in Scottish waters.

Turbot and brill

TURBOT
A popular fish with sea anglers, the turbot is more southern in its distribution than its fellow 'flatties' the plaice, the flounder, and the dab. According to Michael Kennedy (in his book *The Sea Angler's Fishes*), it is common in the Mediterranean, and adjacent Atlantic, west and south of Ireland, in the Channel, in the Irish Sea, and in the southern North Sea, but becomes scarce north of Denmark and is rarely found off the Orkneys and Shetland.

Distribution
From the sea angler's point of view the best hunting grounds for turbot are the large undulating sandbanks off the south and south west coasts – banks like the Varne off Folkestone, the Shambles off Dorset, and the Skerries off Devon. But it is one of sea angling's mysteries why the North Sea, which produces prolific catches of turbot for commercial fishermen, rarely produces fish for rod and line anglers. The biggest turbot ever taken from the east coast was, in fact, a freak 28 lb 8 oz specimen hauled up the beach at Dunwich, Suffolk, by Stowmarket angler Derrick Dorling. This is the present British shore record. More predictable, but still a surprising specimen, was the present British boat record of 32 lb 3 oz, a fish taken by D. Dyer off Plymouth, Devon, in 1976.

Turbot weighing almost 40 lb have, however, been taken aboard commercial vessels operating in Irish waters and with fish over 25 lb regularly falling to rod and line each season the record is certainly far from safe.

Like most species of flat-fish, the princely turbot has both eyes on one side of the body only. The colour of that side varies but is usually brown or grey – the varying density of the colours causing a mottled effect. The opposite, or 'blind' side, is white. The telescopic jaws are armed with numerous sharp teeth.

One of the turbot's most attractive features is that it is never far away from our shorelines, whether it be browsing on the sandbanks or lurking further out in deeper water.

Many people mistakenly believe the turbot to be purely a summer species. This is only because more people fish for them in the summer and because the weather allows anglers to get out on the right marks more consistently than in winter. Therefore it follows that more turbot are caught at this time of year. But turbot do not 'migrate' in the strictest sense of the word and sustained efforts would certainly produce fish in the winter. Turbot favour sandy ground such as the aforementioned banks, but they do tend to move their positions on the banks according to the tide and the colour of the water and sometimes can only be found by experimenting over various sections on a bank.

Tackle and methods

As with most types of fishing, the best way of catching turbot is the simplest. A single size 5/0 hook on a short three- to four-foot long flowing trace is all that is required under most conditions likely to be encountered. Alternatively two baits can be presented on a variation of the old type spreader rig (see figures 12a and 12b).

The turbot is almost entirely a fish-eater – hence that big mouth full of sharp teeth. Its staple diet comprises sand-eels and sprats, but pouting, whiting, herring, bream, and small flat-fish are also eaten, along with other small species. It follows that mackerel strip, presented so that the thinly cut flesh will move invitingly in the tide, is probably the top turbot bait. Sand-eel is also an excellent bait, especially when split down the middle and presented in similar fashion to a fish strip. It is unusual for turbot to be caught on either lugworm or ragworm.

The turbot's jaws can unfold in telescopic fashion to engulf quite a sizeable bait and in doing so the fish registers quite a pronounced bite. But it is important to understand how a turbot takes a bait to achieve maximum success in the hooking of fish. The first sign of a bite will be a short, sharp tap, or perhaps two,

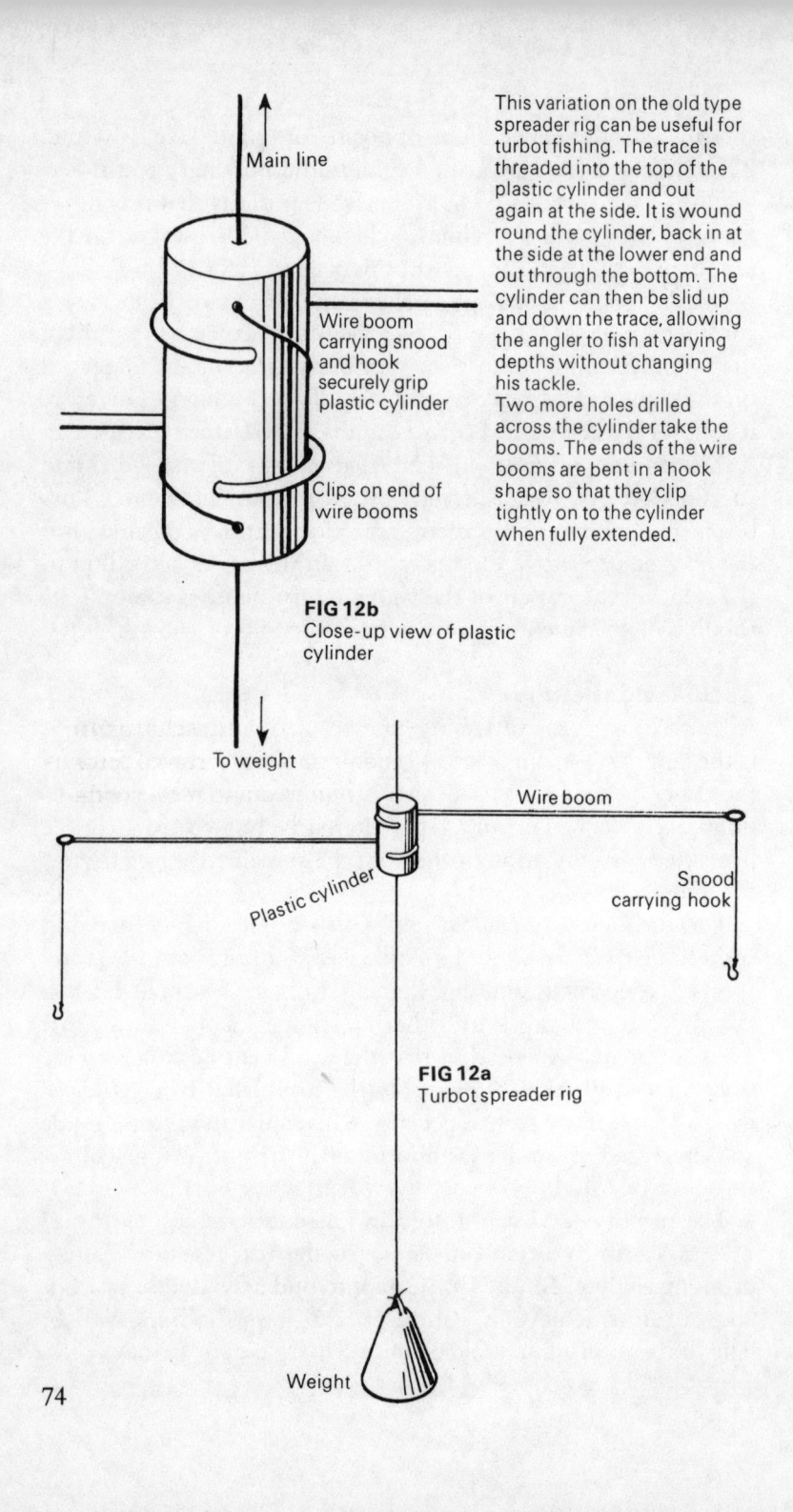

This variation on the old type spreader rig can be useful for turbot fishing. The trace is threaded into the top of the plastic cylinder and out again at the side. It is wound round the cylinder, back in at the side at the lower end and out through the bottom. The cylinder can then be slid up and down the trace, allowing the angler to fish at varying depths without changing his tackle.

Two more holes drilled across the cylinder take the booms. The ends of the wire booms are bent in a hook shape so that they clip tightly on to the cylinder when fully extended.

FIG 12b
Close-up view of plastic cylinder

FIG 12a
Turbot spreader rig

on the rod top. But after this first revelation of its presence the turbot will be quite content to lie motionless on the bottom while gorging a bait. It is most unusual for this fish to run with the bait, as is the case with plaice, for instance.

It is wise to drop the rod top and to wait a few seconds after those first tell-tale taps of the turbot before lifting the weight off the bottom, feeling the weight of the fish, and firmly, but not too sharply, pulling the hook into the fish's jaw. A turbot's mouth is tender inside and a sharp strike can easily tear the hook out completely.

Similarly it pays to play a turbot firmly but with care. Many good fish have been lost by anglers trying to bully them to the surface. Coax the fish slowly upwards and it will usually swim uptide to the surface, making the angler's job a relatively easy one. If you put too much pressure on the fish, it has a habit of lying broadside on against the tide, giving the angler a real problem as he struggles to persuade it back up the tide.

Beach fishing is not nearly as productive as boat fishing for catching turbot, due basically to the fact that the turbot's favourite haunts, such as the sand banks, are well out of reach of even the best beach caster. They can be caught from the shore, however, and Dungeness in Kent and Chesil in Dorset are two examples of areas which, each year, produce occasional specimens. In fact there is probably more chance of turbot being caught from beaches than most anglers realise. Few anglers fish for them from the beach, therefore few are caught. Turbot caught from the beach are normally in the 8 lb to 12 lb range but the 28½-pounder from Dunwich, mentioned earlier, shows just what can be done. Turbot are likely to move inshore to feed on the incoming shoals of sprats in late winter and early spring and returns would be increased if more perseverance was shown at this time of year. Most shore fishermen, however, are preoccupied with cod during this period.

Wrecks too can be productive turbot fishing marks. The fish do not live and feed in the wreck itself, as do conger, ling, coalfish, and pollack, but thrive on nearby sand banks created by the action of the tide on the wreck. The tide, diverted by the bulk of the wreck, scours out the surrounding sand and deposits it in banks close by. These banks are quickly populated by turbot which in turn add another aspect to the wreck fisherman's sport.

The previous British boat record aptly illustrates the potential of turbot fishing over wrecks. The 31 lb 4 oz monster was pulled from the wreck of the 1,000-ton Norwegian cargo ship *The Lab* off Plymouth . . . by a schoolboy! Paul Hutchings, of Plymouth, was only 11 years old when the turbot took the mackerel bait he had intended for conger, and that fish fought so hard everyone aboard the boat thought it was a conger at first – which shows just how well a sizeable turbot can fight, especially in a strong tide.

All turbot have one very special quality, whether caught from boat, beach, or wreck – they are delicious! Along with brill and sole, turbot fetch the highest prices on the fish market.

BRILL

The brill could almost be described as a smaller version of the turbot. It is very similar in general appearance, it is found on the same type of ground, and also shares the turbot's staple diet of sand-eels and sprats. But that is as far as the similarity goes. For the brill does not rate alongside other members of the flat-fish family as a target for anglers – basically because it is not as widespread as the others. Though brill would not be classified as a rarity they are by no means common, only about half a dozen being recorded by anglers each year.

The British boat record is held by A. H. Fisher with a 16 lb specimen he caught off the Isle of Man in 1950. The shore record is held by M. Freeman with a 5 lb 12¼ oz brill caught from Chesil Beach in Dorset. But the biggest fish taken in the past 20 years at least was a 14½-pounder caught from Shoreham Beach by Clemen Melville, of Lindfield, Sussex, in September 1972. Another exceptional specimen taken in recent years was the 13 lb 3¼ oz fish caught by David Berry, of Alderney, Channel Islands, in local waters in October 1974.

Brill, like turbot, are white on the blind side. The other side is generally mottled in different shades of brown, green, or grey and is normally speckled with lighter spots. Brill are also rated highly for their food value.

Bream

Sea anglers are concerned with two types of bream: the red bream and the black bream. Unfortunately both species are limited in their distribution and particular areas along the southern coastline have a monopoly on these tenacious little fish. It is a pity they are not more widely spread around our coastline because they are strikingly handsome fish and the light tackle best used to catch them makes a refreshing change from the heavier gear necessary to handle many other species.

RED BREAM
This fish, otherwise known as the common sea bream, is a colourful character. The body is varying shades of red, becoming darker across the back and melting into a shiny pink along the lower flanks and belly. There is a conspicuous black patch on the hunched shoulders and the fish has large eyes which look almost out of proportion with the rest of its body. It also has a large mouth, well armed with sharp teeth, and bright red fins.

Red bream weighing up to 4 lb are not uncommon. Fish over 5 lb are occasionally reported to the angling press but those over 6 lb are truly exceptional fish. The British boat record is held by Plymouth angler B. H. Reynolds who caught a 9 lb 8¾ oz specimen off Mevagissey, Cornwall, in 1974. That was indeed a rare fish, comfortably outstripping the previous best of 7 lb 8 oz caught way back in 1925. *Angling Times* big fish files record a mere handful of fish weighing more than 6 lb caught in the past decade.

Distribution
Red bream are most prolific at the western end of the English Channel, and it is significant that the previous record was also taken from Cornish waters.

Red bream are less plentiful the further you move eastward

and though they have in the past been caught by trawlers in the North Sea they are not a serious angling proposition along the East Anglian or north east coastlines. They are seasonal visitors to our inshore waters, arriving at the middle or end of June and retreating to deeper water at the end of September. Small fish in the half pound category will come in very close and can be caught in shallow water, but the bigger ones prefer to remain in shoals further out and are most abundant in depths from 10 to 20 fathoms.

Red bream can be found on or near rocky ground. They stick close to the bottom as a rule but can be caught off the bottom in the hours of darkness. They are not fussy eaters and their food is made up mainly of shellfish and seaweed, plus small fish.

It is a sad fact that red bream are not as abundant nowadays as they were 20 to 30 years ago, which is possibly due to the effects of trawling, their sensitivity to ever-increasing pollution around our shores, and thoughtless anglers who needlessly kill far too many of them.

BLACK BREAM

This type of bream favours the same type of rocky, weedy ground. They have the same large eye as the red bream but they are 'dumpier' fish altogether. Their colouring is entirely different. The black bream is not actually black but, as the name implies, its general appearance is dark. The body is usually dark, bluish grey, becoming silvery on the lower parts of the flanks and under the belly. The most obvious feature of all is the dark striping across the back of the fish.

The black bream, sometimes known as the 'old wife', does not grow as big as the red bream but it is a game little fellow and is regarded as the better fighter of the two. Fish of 3 lb are common, anything over 4 lb is good, and a black bream over 5 lb is outstanding. The boat record stands at 6 lb 14¼ oz and the shore record at 4 lb 14¼ oz, both fish being taken in 1977.

Distribution

Unlike red bream, these fish are concentrated towards the eastern end of the Channel, particularly along the Sussex coast where

Littlehampton is probably the chief black bream fishing centre. They are localised species and are again scarce in the North Sea, and are rarely taken in Irish waters.

Black bream appear inshore as early as April, though they usually arrive in most regions in early May. Their departure varies according to locality but is normally during late summer. They search out the rocky, weedy ground in shallow to moderate depths. Their food comprises mainly weed and the organisms found within it, along with small animals such as worms and shrimps.

Tackle and methods
Since red and black bream favour similar types of ground, do not vary considerably in size, and are apt to take the same baits, they can be considered together when it comes to tackle and methods for catching them. Like so many of the smaller species of sea fish, they can provide excellent sport on the right kind of tackle.

Bream fishing is best done from an anchored boat. They do not venture far enough inshore to be reached from the beach and are caught only very rarely from rocks and piers. Therefore, a light, eight-foot rod will serve the purpose admirably. In fact many bream anglers do not use sea fishing rods but prefer a freshwater rod of the type used for catching carp or spinning for pike. The soft action of these light rods will guarantee the angler maximum sport from his fish. Some anglers go to the extreme and use very light fly fishing rods. A 3 lb bream will fight like fury on this sort of tackle.

Since there are no heavy leads to cast when bream fishing, as is the case when beach casting, it is also possible to match the rod with a light line. A 12 lb line, loaded on to a small multiplying reel, is ideal.

The levels at which bream feed vary according to the tide. Black bream prefer to feed when the tide is flowing and under these conditions they will rise up to mid-water and closer to the surface. But at slack water they will move closer to the sea bed. As explained, red bream tend to hug the bottom during the day, but move up in the water as it begins to get dark.

Taking into account that black bream feed in the tide, a normal running leger incorporating a long trace to flow out attractively in the tide is a good rig with which to catch them (see figure 13). Red bream can also be taken in this manner, especially when they begin to move off the bottom. The amount of lead used does, of course, depend on the strength of the tide, though a light line does minimise the amount of weight required because it provides less resistance to the tide. The rule here is to use as little as possible – in fact just enough to slant the line down towards the sea bed in the run of the tide. It is rarely necessary to use more than a couple of ounces. Allow the weight to bump on the bottom and then take in a few turns of line so that the tackle is trotted out in the tide. After that the angler can repeatedly take in or pay out more line so that he is searching out various depths of water and keeping his bait on the move, the latter being important when fishing for bream.

A conventional paternoster will also catch both species of bream and is particularly effective when the fish are close to the bottom. It must, of course, be a single hook affair. There is no room for multi-hook rigs when catching bream. Only the most unsporting of anglers would resort to them. When using a paternoster, attach the weight at the end of the reel line and the snood

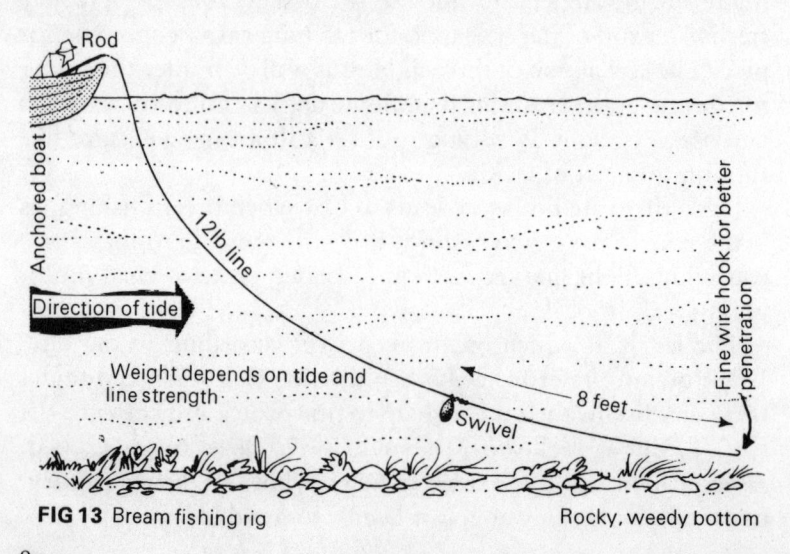

FIG 13 Bream fishing rig

and hook about three feet above the weight. You can then bump the weight on the bottom knowing the baited hook is safely clear of the rocks but still under the noses of the browsing bream.

Hooks should be kept small. Neither species of bream has a large mouth and it is wise here to dip into the freshwater tackle box again. Freshwater hook sizes 2, 4, and 6 should cover any eventuality.

Bream baits are numerous. They will take strips of fish, particularly mackerel, plus ragworm and lugworm, squid, mussels, and a number of other offerings. It pays to remember, however, that bream are the biggest bait robbers in the business. They are experts at removing the bait from the hook and avoiding being caught. The secret of foiling the wily bream lies in bait presentation. A strip of mackerel hooked at one end only, so that it flows out in the current, is simply inviting the fish to take it without being hooked. But by threading a four-inch fish strip on the hook three or four times, the bream will find that he cannot pull it off and has to chew the bait. In this way he takes the hook well in his mouth, giving the angler a good chance of hooking him.

When a bream takes the bait properly it usually produces a good, bold bite. Ignore the initial knocks and wait until the bream pulls the rod top firmly round before lifting the rod sharply over the shoulder in a smooth, firm strike. It is a good idea to tie a small piece of elasticated cotton on the line between the reel and butt ring. When a fish is caught it is possible to return the bait to the same depth on the next cast by making sure the marker is in the same position. For if you catch one bream, you have undoubtedly located a shoal. Groundbaiting will help you hold them there. Fill a mesh bag with mashed-up fish mixed with pilchard oil and suspend it in the tide from the anchor rope. The mixture will be washed down the same line of the tide as your bait.

The safest and simplest way of bringing bream aboard a boat is with a landing net, and any fish not required for the pot – three or four are ample for any angler – should be returned to the water. Too many anglers have been pictured posing proudly with scores of dead bream at their feet. No wonder this species is in decline around our coasts. The senseless killing of bream by anglers is a terrible waste of a wonderfully sporting fish.

The Ray's bream is an unusual visitor to our waters and is not regarded as a serious quarry by rod and line anglers. Only occasionally is it caught by angling methods and then merely by coincidence. These fish have been known to turn up in the trawl nets of commercial fishermen and now and again they are found washed up on our beaches, for they are not really suited to the conditions around these shores.

A deep-bodied but not very thick fish, the Ray's bream has a silvery-grey, almost metallic, appearance and a large eye. It is believed to swim at considerable depths for much of its life.

Despite its rarity, the Ray's bream is included in the British Record (rod-caught) Fish List. G. Walker earned that distinction when he landed a 7 lb 15¾ oz fish at Crimdon Beach, Hartlepool, in 1967. The committee are awaiting claims for a boat record, having set a minimum qualifying weight of 5 lb.

Those fluke fish caught on rod and line around the British Isles normally come from the east coast. *Angling Times* files record only four fish during 1971. Two came from Norfolk, one from Yorkshire and one from Durham. The north east coast seems particularly productive for this species. Several have been taken in this area in recent years and G. Walker's record fish was soon followed by a 6 lb 3 oz specimen from the Tyne Estuary.

The south coast also has its share. Of the three Ray's bream recorded during 1969, one came from the Sussex coast, one from Somerset and the other from Yorkshire. Those caught are normally over 5 lb, but dead fish weighing up to 14 lb have been found on the shoreline.

Tope

This fish is sometimes referred to as the poor man's shark. A tigerish species, it resembles a small shark in appearance and is of the same predatory nature. But it is a sporting fish in its own right and will more often than not put up a better fight than a shark of similar size. Indeed, the tope is one of the fastest fighters in the sea. Its streamlined body and big tail are ideally suited to speed and a full-blooded tope run is something to be experienced. The fish will pick up a bait and tear off at a terrific speed and it is certainly not advisable to try to stop a tope at this stage!

Distribution
This exciting predator is among the most popular of sea fish, basically because of its widespread distribution. The tope is caught from John O'Groats to Land's End – literally. The Mull of Galloway on the west coast of Scotland, the East Anglian Wash, and the Welsh coast are all prolific areas for catching tope. Big tope are also regularly taken in Irish waters, but the present British boat record is held with a fish of 74 lb 11 oz taken off Caldy Island, off the Pembrokeshire coast, in 1964. In sharp contrast, the best ever shore-caught fish, a 54 lb 4 oz specimen, was taken from Loch Ryan in Wigtownshire, in 1975. The captor was D. Hastings.

The first tope of the year are normally moving inshore around most parts of the country by April, for they are basically a summer species and are regarded as a good proposition until September or October. This, at least, is the seasonal rule which governs most tope anglers. But Ack Harries, the British boat record holder from Saundersfoot, Pembrokeshire, contends that tope are an all-the-year-round species which remain within reach of the angler even during the winter. Ack maintains that tope remain relatively close inshore during the colder months, not just off his native Welsh coast but also in other coastal regions.

He argues that the reason few tope are caught during the winter is because no one bothers to fish for them. Ack himself has caught tope around the 60 lb mark on Christmas Day in past years and offers that as proof of his theory. Despite this unexploited winter potential, spring is the best time for really big tope. The females carry their young during April and May and this can add another 20 lb or 30 lb to a big fish. Almost all big tope are females, whereas males rarely exceed 40 lb. Fortunately for the angler females show a distinct preference for shallow water, while the males are found further offshore in deeper water.

Tope hunt in packs, searching out mackerel, dabs, and bream close to the sea bed. Traditionally they are regarded as a boat-caught species, though in recent years the popularity of shore fishing for tope has increased tremendously, particularly in Devon and Cornwall. The great advantage of boat fishing is that it allows the angler to search out the tope's favourite ground – namely the inshore gullies which drop down deeper than the surrounding sea bed. These gullies, which may drop down another three to four fathoms in depth, can be found within half a mile of the shore. Tope run up the pebbles and shingle on the bottom of the gullies to clean themselves, so the bait needs to be right down in the bottom of the trough.

Tackle

When it comes to selecting terminal tackle, you cannot beat a straightforward long flowing trace, incorporating a wire trace. The length of wire used in the rig depends on the angler himself, the problem being that tope tend to twist and roll up in the trace and either bite through the nylon above or chafe it to breaking point on their rough skin.

Therefore it can be fatal to use a very short trace. One answer to the problem, however, is to use a fairly short length of wire, two feet for example, with a longer nylon trace directly above it (see figure 14). The weight is attached above the nylon trace. A nylon trace of about 70 lb breaking strain is tough enough to withstand the chafing effect of the tope's skin and fins. Alternatively, a much longer wire trace is favoured by some tope experts. Ack Harries, for example, uses 18 feet of 35 lb single strand wire and claims to have never lost a tope as a result of the fish biting the line above the trace!

The basic tope fisherman's tackle is completed by a 35 lb main line, a size 10/0 hook, and a weight which varies according to the strength of the tide. A moving bait helps to attract a hunting tope and for this reason the weight should be just enough to hold the bait down. A slight raising and lowering of the rod top will then allow you to bounce the weight around and work the bait over fresh ground. A 2 oz weight is fine when you can get away with it but when the tide is running hard down those gullies, 1 lb 8 oz of lead may be necessary.

Baits

Mackerel is without a doubt the top bait for tope, accounting for far more fish than any other bait. Fresh bait is essential. The tope is a hunting fish and will show little interest in a stale offering. Anglers in search of very big tope will often use whole mackerel, but more tope are taken on a side of mackerel or a thick fillet presented to flutter attractively in the tide. There are a number of other good tope baits, though in many cases their effectiveness varies according to the areas in which they are used. Small dabs about the size of the palm of your hand are a favourite bait off certain areas of the Welsh coast and small live bream account for big tope in the Solent. Similarly squid is a good bait in the West Country and pouting is always a good general standby when mackerel is not available.

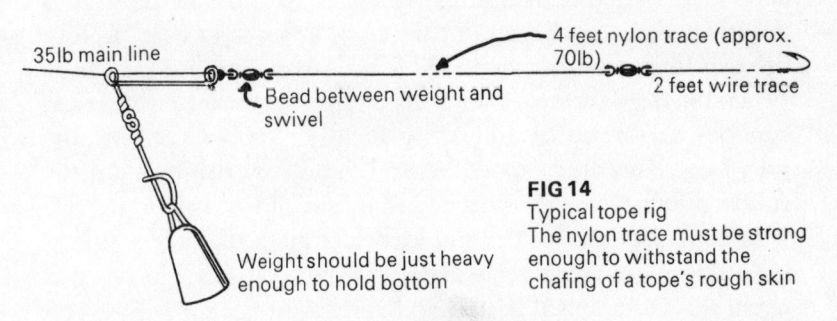

FIG 14
Typical tope rig
The nylon trace must be strong enough to withstand the chafing of a tope's rough skin

(35lb main line — Bead between weight and swivel — 4 feet nylon trace (approx. 70lb) — 2 feet wire trace; Weight should be just heavy enough to hold bottom)

Methods

There is no mistaking a tope bite. There may be a jerk on the line as the fish grabs at the bait, and this will normally be followed by a searing run. If you are using a multiplier reel leave it out of gear when waiting for a fish to take, and use your thumb to prevent an over-run when a tope streaks off with the bait. The tope may only be gripping the bait loosely at first so do not set the hook until it has had sufficient time to get both the bait and the hook well inside its mouth. And it is no use tightening the drag on the reel once the fish is hooked. The tope will want to run and dive, and if the fish is of any size there is nothing you can do about it. Just concentrate on keeping a tight line, to prevent the fish rolling up the trace, until the tope is tired enough to coax towards the boat. Use a light rod about nine feet long and even a small tope will give a fight not easily forgotten.

Tope caught from the shore take a bait in a similar fashion and the fight can be even more hectic in the shallower water. A conventional leger rig, incorporating a weight balanced to provide a little movement across the tide, again takes some beating. A longer rod of the beachcasting variety is required when fishing from the beach in order to cast the necessary distance.

One of the advantages of boat fishing is that tope can be attracted to the vicinity of your bait by the use of rubby dubby, the sea angler's term for groundbait. And those gullies make great channels for a rubby dubby trail. The contents of rubby dubby are mashed up fish and any rejected scraps of bait left lying around the boat. In fact just about anything goes in and it can be a messy business – but it does not have to be! A clean and efficient method is to mince the fish up at home, put it into polythene bags, and then put the bags in a deep freeze. Before the fish freezes push a stick and length of string into each bag. When the bags are frozen solid all smells are eliminated and each bag can be carried by the string handle. Aboard the boat the polythene bags are stripped off and the frozen fish put into the rubby dubby net. It is simple, clean, and, most important, effective. It also lasts longer and leaves a longer trail in the water. If you need convincing, just bear in mind that Ack Harries was using this tactic when he caught his record tope.

The best conditions for tope are hot days and evenings and flat calms. Rough weather does not produce as many fish, probably because they do not have very good eyesight and cannot spot a bait as well in a dirty sea. Even in ideal conditions and armed with the right tackle and bait, tope fishing can be a waiting game. A whole day's fishing without a run is by no means rare. But the thrills and spills of catching tope make all the waiting worthwhile – especially on occasions like that experienced by Hastings, Sussex, angler Jack Reece on a summer's day in 1974.

Jack, who was fishing in the European Tope Championship in Cardigan Bay off the Welsh coast, literally caught too many tope. Fishing with his brother Peter aboard his boat *Shikari*, Jack caught 16 tope. Peter added another seven and they hauled so many aboard that the weight threatened to sink the boat. For by this time the gunnels of the *Shikari* were dangerously close to the water. So Jack took the only course open to him – he jettisoned six of his fish! Fortunately the gamble paid off. *Shikari* made it safely back to port and Jack retained the title he had won the previous year with his remaining 10 tope weighing a total of 319 lb. The brothers' combined catch scaled a magnificent 516 lb 8 oz.

Dogfish

Pests, vermin, scavengers . . . those are just a few of the adjectives used to describe the dogfish, a sleek, predatory species resembling the tope in appearance. It is little more than a nuisance fish both to the sea angler and the commercial fisherman. It will take any bait offered it, drive other fish out of the area, and attack and tear nets. There is little skill needed to catch the dogfish. It will hook itself and put up a poor fight. It is an acceptable though not especially tasty table fish.

The dogfish is, however, very widely distributed throughout British waters and is particularly prolific along the south coast and in Scottish waters. Five dogfish (or closely related species) are recognised by the British Record (rod-caught) Fish Committee: the spurdog, the lesser spotted dogfish, the bull huss, the smoothhound and the black-mouthed dogfish.

SPURDOG

These greedy fish are the most common, and most troublesome, of the dogfish. They hunt in huge packs, roaming all levels of water from the surface to the sea bed, and are found in up to 70 fathoms. Their natural food includes mackerel, herring, pilchards, whiting, flat-fish, and gurnards. They will take just about any bait and often attack other fish when they are being reeled in. When hooked they make a few short, zig-zag runs but soon submit.

It is difficult to think of any points in the spurdog's favour, though it is fair to say that it makes up some big weights in competition fishing, particularly in Scotland, and it fills in a gap for the angler along the south coast before other fish such as bass, thornback, and tope move inshore.

Anyone inclined to fish seriously for spurdog is best advised to use fairly light tackle. A light boat rod with a 15 lb line will do the job nicely and a single hook flowing trace will give the fish maximum opportunity to give a good account of itself. A wire trace is necessary because the spurdog's sharp teeth will soon cut through nylon. Spurdog bites are very definite and almost impossible to miss, but beware the spines on the dorsal fin when unhooking the fish.

The British record for spurdog stands at 21 lb 3 oz 7 dr (boat-caught) and 16 lb 12½ oz (shore-caught).

LESSER SPOTTED DOGFISH
This is a much smaller member of the dogfish family, the shore record standing at only 4 lb 8 oz and the boat record at 4 lb 1 oz 13 dr. Again it has a wide distribution, preferring sandy or muddy bottoms, and is only of nuisance value to anglers. It usually feeds close to the sea bed, taking in crustaceans such as crabs and shrimps along with worms, sand-eels, and small fish. Virtually any bait will lead to its downfall.

BULL HUSS
Also known as the greater spotted dogfish, this fish is broader and heavier than its lesser spotted 'cousin'. It is distinguishable by the large spots on its body and, although it is found all around our coast, it is not as prolific as the spurdog. It prefers deeper water and rougher ground than the lesser spotted dogfish. It eats crustaceans and small fish and has been known to take lesser spotted dogfish. The British boat record, held with a fish of 21 lb 3 oz, has stood since 1955. The shore record of 17 lb 15 oz was set up in 1977 by M. Roberts. He caught his fish at Trefusis Point, Cornwall.

SMOOTHHOUND
This fish runs to larger sizes, the record being 28 lb. It moves out into deeper water during the winter so it is usually caught in the summer months. The smoothhound's diet consists of crustaceans – mainly crabs – and worms.

Shark

These are the most 'romantic' of all fish. They hold a special magic not only with anglers but with anyone who has heard of their 'man-eating' reputation. The thought of a shark's dorsal fin carving across the surface of the water or of that spine-chilling, low-slung jaw armed with serrated teeth immediately stirs the imagination. The shark has all the qualities needed to make it a sporting proposition. Most important it is a big fish, but it is also a very fast and furious fighter. Certain species of shark are distributed all around our coasts and they are not particularly difficult to catch.

It is no wonder then that anglers on these islands have fished for them for over 100 years. Our best shark waters are in the Channel, particularly off the Devon and Cornwall coasts and around the Isle of Wight. The west coast of Ireland is a prolific area and they can also be caught in Scottish waters, a fact highlighted by Dr Dietrich Burkel when he caught a 173 lb 10 oz specimen in the Mull of Galloway off the coast of Scotland in August 1970. The full potential of shark fishing in Scottish waters has yet to be realised, however.

Boat owners have cashed in on the attraction of the shark and shark fishing charter trips are big business at West Country sea fishing centres during the summer. In addition to the trips made by serious shark anglers, holidaymakers, who do not normally go fishing, can hire tackle and bait for day trips after shark.

Blue shark are the most common of the shark family, but there are three other types which are of interest to the angler – namely porbeagle, thresher, and mako.

BLUE SHARK

This is the most common of the shark and like the others is caught during the summer months. It tends to run to a smaller average size than the rest and the British boat record of 218 lb

– a fish caught off Looe, Cornwall, in 1959 by N. Sutcliffe – is the lowest of the four records. The world record blue shark weighed 410 lb when caught at Rockport, Massachusetts, in 1960 but it is unlikely that fish approaching such a weight will be caught in British waters.

The average weight of blue shark caught off the West Country is about 50 lb, though 100 lb fish are not rare. The small class of fish can be caught in large numbers, though the tackle on which they are taken is normally far too heavy. This is certainly true in the case of charter trips run for holidaymakers where the prime concerns are for the customer to get a shark on the deck and not to lose the tackle.

As its name implies, the blue shark is easily distinguishable by its colour. The back of the fish is dark blue and this fades into a watery blue on the flanks. The belly is white. The fish arrives in British waters by June where it remains until October. Mackerel is its chief food though it also takes herring, pilchards, and other fish; even seagulls have been found in its stomach.

PORBEAGLE SHARK

The next type of shark most commonly caught on rod and line is the porbeagle. It is of a higher average weight than the blue shark and the best taken from British waters is a 465-pounder caught off Padstow, Cornwall, in 1976 by Jorge Potier.

An altogether chunkier fish than the slimline blue, the porbeagle is also a much harder fighter. It is fairly common in Cornish waters and has been caught commercially in the North Sea. It is also found on the west and south coasts of Ireland but rarely moves inshore in these areas. *Angling Times* files reveal that the waters surrounding the Isle of Wight emerged as excellent grounds for porbeagle around 1970. A spate of fish over 150 lb were taken there at the time and this trend has continued. However, the Padstow area is now favourite to produce big porbeagles following a spate of fish from this region in recent years.

Off Cornwall and the Isle of Wight the porbeable swim closer inshore than the blue shark and it has even been caught from the beach. Though this is a rare occurrence it is a useful pointer for boat anglers who should pay attention to the relatively shallow water rather than the far-off deeps. The porbeagle swims at varying levels in the water but feeds mainly on the bottom on such fish as cod and bream as well as feasting among shoals of mackerel and herring. Colour-wise, the porbeagle has a bluish grey or browny back with a white belly.

THRESHER SHARK

The thresher shark – so called because of its tremendously long and oddly shaped tail which it uses to lash the water when 'rounding-up' small shoals of fish to eat – is rarely caught on rod and line in British waters. The British Record (rod-caught) Fish Committee do, however, recognise the species and the record is held with a 280 lb fish caught by H. A. Kelly at Dungeness, Kent, in 1933. One of the rare thresher shark taken on rod and line in recent years was a 156 lb specimen caught by David Thomas, of New Malden, Surrey, while fishing off Gosport in Hampshire.

The only reason that so few threshers are caught in our waters would seem to be that few people know anything about them and, as a result, they are rarely fished for. They are regular summer visitors to the West Country coastline and have been taken in nets on other parts of the coast. There is no reason to suspect that they are a particularly rare species of shark in British waters. Mackerel, herring, and pilchards make up their staple diet.

MAKO SHARK

It is impossible to talk about the mako shark without recalling one of the most incredible catches in the history of angling. The 'fairy tale' began on a May day in 1971 when Norwich grandmother Joyce Yallop set out from Looe, Cornwall, on a charter fishing trip aboard *Lady Betty* skippered by Alan Dingle. The anglers aboard were feathering for pollack as *Lady Betty* drifted in the tide four miles north west of the famous Eddystone Reef, when skipper Alan spotted a huge fin slicing lazily through the water some way off. At first Alan thought the fish was a basking shark, but when he cut his motors to take a better look he realised it was a giant mako.

Immediately Joyce, then aged 61, insisted on trying to catch the massive fish as it cruised along in search of food. Borrowing a shark rod, she baited with a whole mackerel and tossed the offering out towards the shark. The bait was taken and a battle which was to last a full two-and-a-half hours began.

Time after time Joyce – her hands sore, her wrist bruised by the reel and her body bruised by the straining harness – hauled the fish close to the boat and the waiting gaff. But each time it streaked away, tearing nearly 300 yards of 130 lb line from the reel. Joyce, crying from exhaustion, never gave up. Encouraged by skipper Alan, she eventually managed to coax the shark close enough for him to sink the gaff and lash the fish to the side of the boat. Joyce, who runs a tea stall in Norwich market, broke down in a state of collapse. But she had boated the heaviest shark – it weighed 500 lb – ever taken on rod and line in European waters and became the new holder of the British record for mako shark.

The feat was a truly remarkable one. For the mako is the hardest fighting, largest, and most sought-after shark available to the British angler. It is a fast, active fish and will often jump clear of the water in a frenzied bid for freedom when hooked. Joyce's fish not only leapt out of the water but twice charged the boat during the fight!

Mako were at one time mistaken for porbeagle and it was only in the late 1950s, when shark fishing began to emerge as a more specialised aspect of angling, that they were identified as a separate species. They are found mostly off Cornwall and, up until now, have been exclusive to West Country waters. Mako of up to 1,000 lb are believed to swim in these waters. The biggest mako ever recorded weighed 1,000 lb and was taken at Mayor Island, New Zealand, in 1943. The mako is blue in colour and is stouter then the blue shark, though not as stout as the porbeagle.

Tackle

The strength of the tackle used to catch shark depends, of course, on which particular species you wish to fish for. A rod and line suited to fishing for mako would, for instance, be far too heavy for catching blue shark. But there are some general rules worth following.

Solid fibreglass is accepted as the best material for rods. Though it is heavier than hollow glass, it is more durable and can stand up better to the pressures imposed on it by shark fishing. Roller rings minimise the amount of wear on the line and this should be borne in mind. Some rods have a roller ring only at the tip, the other rings being of the fixed type. It is best to obtain a rod with roller rings throughout if a great amount of shark fishing is to be done. A rod of this type can be bought for around £15, although the very good ones are much more expensive.

There is really only one type of reel worth using for shark fishing – the multiplier. A large capacity multiplier capable of carrying at least 300 yards of strong line is essential and again this should cost in the region of £15.

Braided, rot-proof line is expensive, but it is worth paying the extra if it means the difference between landing and losing a fish. The line must also float because shark fishing incorporates the use of a float and the angler may have to take a large amount of line off the water on the strike. A line lying below the water will take the punch out of the strike and make it almost impossible to set the hook. Stretchy lines are of little use for the same reason. They take impact and penetration out of the strike.

Strength of line and choice of hooks also depends on the size of fish the angler is likely to catch. A line of 50 lb breaking strain is fine for blue shark but inadequate for porbeagle and mako. Lines from 80 lb to 120 lb breaking strain are better for the heavier types of shark. Similarly a 10/0 hook is plenty big enough for blue shark but it is wise to step up to 14/0 or 16/0 for its big brothers. The size of the bait must also be taken into account.

Boats which specialise in the holidaymaker trade through the summer season usually have complete sets of tackle already made up for hire. These are almost always far too heavy, especially considering blue shark are the quarry. Shark fishing gives the angler plenty of scope to make his own tackle. Wire traces, an essential part of the equipment due to the shark's sharp teeth and rough skin, can be made up much more cheaply than they can be bought. Spools of nylon-covered wire can be bought from any good tackle shop. It is a simple matter to attach your own swivels, though remember to crimp them on rather than twist the wire. Twisting will severely weaken the trace. Traces should be of 120 lb breaking strain and at least 12 feet long to ensure against the shark rolling up in the trace and biting through the nylon.

Floats can also be made easily at home. Detergent bottles or big corks make excellent sliding floats once you have attached a swivel at one end. Some anglers also use small balloons. They are easy to see a long way off and provide movement to the bait as they are carried along by the wind.

Baits

Mackerel is by far the best shark bait. It can be used in several ways, all of which proved effective at one time or another. The simplest way of baiting with a single mackerel is to hook it once through the wrist of the tail. This is the firmest part of the fish's body and the bait is unlikely to come off. If you have doubts, secure it further by tying the shank of the hook to the tail with a few turns of elasticated cotton. Using this method it is also convenient to bait with two mackerel at once. The bony skull of the mackerel is also a good hooking area. The hook can be passed through the eye sockets or through the snout of the fish. Alternatively, some anglers prefer to thread the mackerel, putting the hook in at the vent or nearer the tail so that the point protrudes from the back.

Locating the depth at which shark are feeding is usually a case of trial and error. When the first shark of the day is boated it is normal for the rest of the anglers aboard to adjust their floats to the depth at which the fish was hooked.

There is no mistaking a shark bite. The float will sometimes plunge out of sight never to reappear, while at other times it will bob sharply below the surface two or three times before vanishing. The star drag on the multiplier should be left in the off position so that the fish feels no resistance when it runs. The rod could also be pulled overboard if the drag is left on. The timing of the strike is largely a matter of experience. Do not rush the strike but wait until you are confident the fish has the bait well into his mouth. Even experienced anglers lose fish on the strike.

Playing big shark requires the use of a shoulder harness which incorporates a butt pad into which the rod butt is placed. There are also two shoulder straps which clip on to the sides of the reel. The gaffing of a shark is normally left to the skipper who fastens his gaffs securely to the boat in case a fish should break away with a gaff still attached. But the fight does not end when the fish is in the boat. Shark will leap about and can be dangerous. A hard blow on the snout with a mallet is the best way of killing them.

The use of rubby dubby is an essential part of shark fishing. Mashed-up stale fish mixed with pilchard oil is put into a mesh sack and this is hung over the side. The fish slick will be carried downtide for several miles as the boat drifts along and will attract shark to the boat. Shark fishing is rarely done at anchor.

Conger

Newcomers to conger fishing might be excused, if they glance at recent records, for thinking that this important and popular aspect of sea fishing did not begin until the late 1960s. Since the beginning of what may safely be called the wreck fishing revolution, rod and line catches of conger eels have multiplied many times. In 1933 H. A. Kelly caught an 84 lb conger while fishing offshore from Dungeness and his record stood for 37 years. That record was first beaten in 1970 . . . and in the seven seasons since then has been humbled many times. The record weight climbed progressively to 109 lb 6 oz and such has been the scale of big conger catches that 60-pounders are no longer considered anything very special when wreck fishing.

A number of quite separate happenings and discoveries provided the impetus for the transition. One of the most important, even though it came with the growing popularity of conger fishing and was not in itself a prime reason for the boom, was the formation of the British Conger Club. This organisation is freely hailed as the best of the organisations devoted to a single species. Membership now approaches 1,000 and continues to expand. The club organises both localised and nationwide contests involving fishing for conger eels and much of its progress can be credited to secretary, Reg Quest, 5 Hill Crest, Mannamead, Plymouth, and other efficient officials.

However the first breakthrough in conger fishing came with the realisation that Decca Navigator equipment could be used in conjunction with echo-sounders to locate deep water wrecks situated far from land. This Decca equipment had previously been used by trawlermen to locate wrecks simply to avoid the resultant damage to their nets if these fouled on underwater obstructions. Now it is working the other way around and a great variety of sunken ships of all sizes, scattered conveniently off the British shoreline, have become hotspots of great value.

Until the application of Decca equipment, wreck fishermen had been limited to fishing hulks lying in relatively shallow water, the exact location of the hull being revealed by the turbulence of the sea downtide of the wreck (see figure 15). The deflection of the tide by inshore wrecks is clearly visible, particularly when anglers have the benefit of shore bearings to guide them to the approximate location. So it became possible to locate all known wrecks with Decca. Many others were also discovered as this equipment became more popular and was used in conjuction with echo sounders to locate and chart more and more of these heavily-stocked fish larders.

The Brixham-based *Our Unity* was the most successful boat in the early days, a reputation maintained ever since. Her skipper-owners, Ernie Passmore and John Trust, were popular hard working trawlermen who discovered the pleasures and the demand for wreck fishing and, with it, perfected the necessary technique by which a fishing boat can be anchored to fish wrecks. No easy matter, that, but vital for conger fishing success. In some instances it is as futile to fish 10 yards as 10 miles away from the wreckage. Allowances must be made for veering winds, and the changing pace of the tide but it is perhaps fortunate that

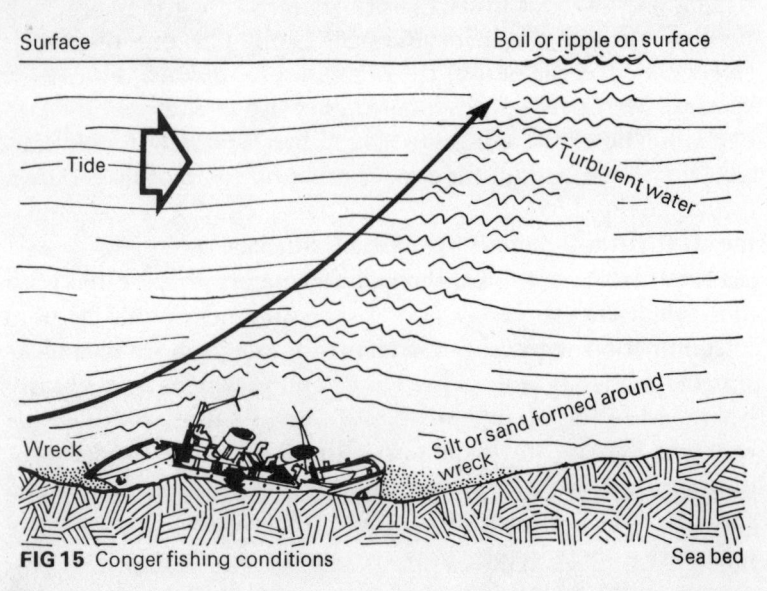

FIG 15 Conger fishing conditions

the best of the sport usually comes when the water is standing and during the periods either side of the top and bottom of each tide.

At one time it was thought that conger eel fishing was necessarily seasonal; that the fish migrated beyond the horizon with the onset of winter. This is not so. Conger eels are susceptible to frost and during the sustained periods of heavy frost in the 1963 winter large numbers were washed ashore dead. They showed in areas where the inshore sea is shallow and, surprisingly, many were seen in areas not renowned for conger eel fishing. That applies in particular to the east coast, generally regarded as poor ground for conger fishing.

The fact that so many eels, including some over 50 lb, died in inshore waters proves the eels do not move so far away as was at one time imagined – if they move at all. Most of the wreck fishing currently underway involves depths of 28 fathoms or more. Frost would be unlikely to affect eels that far from the surface. In truth, the slowdown of winter conger fishing relates rather more to the state of the sea than any lack of eels.

During winter the tides and winds can be much stronger than in summer and it is then more difficult to anchor a fishing boat without it dragging. It is also more difficult for anglers to put their baits down on to the wreck effectively. Even on the better days it is sometimes necessary to fish with as much as 2 lb of lead to hold bottom. More weight makes fishing very hard work and when the conditions are unfavourable most charter boats revert to drift fishing, with the boat being repeatedly taken uptide to drift down over the wreck. The main objective then becomes cod, pollack, and coalfish, for conger do not take very often when the boat is moving.

There is no longer much excitement if a charter boat takes 2,000 lb of conger eels from a single wreck in one day's fishing, but, nevertheless, this is no easy target to achieve. It is nearcertainty that most virgin wrecks are heavily stocked with conger but in most instances they are just as heavily inhabited by ling. Ling are faster to feed than conger eels, with the result that anglers hoping for heavy hauls of eels have first to denude the wreck of its ling. This is usually expected to take up to two days if the wreck is substantial.

A big wreck can produce 1,500 lb of ling averaging around 24 lb each before the conger begin to show in force. But, with the ling disposed of, the conger can then be hit in force. Under good fishing conditions it often proves that as many as six of the 10 anglers aboard can hook conger simultaneously. The small 'strap' conger show first as a rule. They too are quick off the mark and grab the baits before the bigger eels have a chance. But with the number of small eels progressively reduced so the bigger ones begin to feed. The second and third days are usually rated the best for really big eels so, allowing two days to dispose of the ling, it can quickly be seen that a full week's fishing may be necessary before the top quality conger can be contacted.

The economics of charter boat fishing are such that the boat skippers expect substantial income from the sale of the fish their anglers catch. Anglers raise few objections to this. Who wants a 70 lb conger eel to eat anyway? But when the number of conger left on a wreck is sharply reduced then, from the skippers' point of view, the fishing becomes uneconomic. They like mammoth catches of middle-weight eels, but once conger eel fishing becomes a long and drawn out affair of waiting for the really outstanding conger to feed their income suffers. This, in effect, means that many of the offshore wrecks regarded as fished-out still hold their best conger. Many of the eels weighing under 80 lb have been caught but the record breakers, eels weighing over 100 lb, remain.

Conger eels weighing over three figures are an awesome proposition on rod and line. The chances of landing an eel of such proportions cannot be higher than 20–1 against. These eels spend much of their time within the hulk of the wrecks. Thus, when they are hooked they are never far from the ironwork. This makes the first seconds of contact vital. If the eels are given the time to writhe backwards they can either lock themselves around metal or retreat far enough for the line to fray on iron. In either situation the chances of beating the conger are then no better than nil.

To succeed the angler must hit a conger hard from the moment it is first hooked. There must be no slack line – the stretch in monofilament alone could provide those few inches that are sufficient to ensure the conger's safety. An eel must be lifted off the sea bed or wreck fast, so that its flailing tail cannot find a lodging place. Once a big eel is away from the wreck and in snag-free water the angler's chances increase very considerably. Yet the battle will have only just begun. Conger maintain relentless pressure on the tackle and on the angler himself. A big eel can be brought to the surface only for it to make an additional effort, get its head down and tail up, and zoom all the way down to the depths once more. The strain on the tackle is immense, but the eel must be prevented from reaching the wreck at all costs for once back there the fight is over. If one of these power dives is defeated this can be expected again, and again, before a really big conger is beaten.

Even with the conger on the surface within gaffing range the fight cannot be counted as won. Eighty pounds of whipping writhing conger is not easily lifted out of sea. Boatmen usually apply two gaffs to big eels, one just behind the head, the other mid-way along the body and once two gaffs are in then the two boatmen have the situation under control. But big eels have been known to twist off a gaff, inflicting great injury on themselves but nevertheless finally breaking free.

This is hard, exacting fishing, exhausting too, and, in the heat of the action, which always shows when the heavy catches are made, many an experienced conger fisherman has secretly hoped for a respite. Fortunately the conger usually comes in waves. Once the first has been dealt with there will be a lull before the next batch arrives, probably scenting the fish baits and blood and moving in from other sections of the wreck.

The boatman must constantly assess the power of the tide in relation to the strength and direction of the wind. Slight variations alone are enough to move the boat far enough for the anglers' baits to be dropping clear of the wreck where the bigger eels will ignore them.

It may be necessary first to progressively 'search' the wreck to locate the conger and then to adjust the position of the boat two or even three times in each six-hour tide to maintain contact.

When the action is at a peak, lost baits, blood, and guts flow freely and there are times when porbeagle and blue sharks are attracted to add another ingredient to the fury.

Distribution
This large-scale wreck fishing is at present mainly confined to the lower sections of the English Channel, principally off Dorset, and south Devon and Cornwall but the wreck boats are venturing further and further afield in this area. They are now fishing in mid-channel, halfway between France and England, journeys which involve many hours travelling time to and from the wrecks. This has in turn resulted in 36-hour charters. The boats put out from port one day and return on the evening of the next. The anglers thus have the opportunity for increased periods of action, although, in truth, most of them are glad of a night's sleep at sea rather than fishing through the night.

It has been argued that wreck fishing for conger eels requires brute strength and next to no finesse. The sport will never be everyone's ideal, but it is likely to be extended further and further around the coastline as the necessary boats, and, particularly the Decca wreck-locating equipment, become available. This is expensive equipment, involving an annual rental of about £400, plus installation charges, and boatmen, other than those in the West Country, have shown some reticence in using it.

Conger fishing over wrecks is likely to spread next to Yorkshire – out from Whitby, Bridlington, and Scarborough – to Wales and perhaps ultimately to Scotland and Ireland. The coloured sea in the lower sections of the North Sea is believed to have 'sanded' the many wrecks situated there with the result that they are less popular with eels. Wreck fishing is always likely to be most successful in areas where the sea is clean and clear.

There must be mammoth conger along the rocky sections of the Irish coast and although wrecks are likely to prove less numerous here the future must see an extension of eel fishing to this area. The same is true of Scottish waters. Shore fishing for conger is highly productive along many sections of the Scottish mainland, often producing fish as big as, and sometimes bigger than, those caught further south. So Scotland too will join the wreck fishing revolution in due course.

Conger fishing is not, of course, confined to wrecks. There are other situations where it can be productive. Reefs produce many good fish every year, although it must be conceded that these do not yield as many big eels. Reefs are, of course, their natural home with areas of rock and crag frequented by conger of all sizes.

The heaviest reef-caught conger on record is an 89-pounder from the Eddystone, off Plymouth, by J. Jordanopolu in 1936 – an eel never claimed as a British record but which was big enough to have ousted H. A. Kelly's 84-pounder from Dungeness. In recent years 60 lb appears to have been the upper weight limit. Tony Ward-Edwards got one of 59 lb 9 oz from The Rutts, a reef off Plymouth, in 1974 and there have been others well into the 50 lb class.

Reef fishing involves much shallower water than is found over most wrecks. This means that reef-caught eels come to the surface with much more fight left in them than eels hauled up 200 feet from the sea bed. Reefs are not generally quite so snag-ridden as wrecks but rock crevices and gullies can pose problems to anglers who fish with tackle inadequate for the task.

Shore fishing for conger is carried out along many sections of coast where the underwater terrain is suitable for the eels. East coast conger fishing is effectively nil, but the south and south-west coasts are worthwhile prospects in areas where a rocky shoreline and inshore reefs, however small, provide the eels with food and shelter.

The biggest conger so far landed by an angler fishing from the shore is the 67 lb 4 oz eel caught by Albert Lander of Torquay while fishing near Torquay harbour.

Estuaries also contain substantial numbers of conger, some of the best being the Dart, Tamar, and Fowey. In this situation the best catches are usually made after nightfall.

Tackle

This needs to be top quality to stand the strain. Rods with a test curve of 20 lb to 30 lb are generally used, in conjunction with heavy-duty multiplier reels loaded with lines of 50 lb to 70 lb breaking strain. Forged steel hooks of around size 10/0 are normally used and these are fastened to stranded stainless steel traces of 150 lb breaking strain. These traces need be no more than two feet long, just enough to prevent the eel from champing through the nylon monofilament main line. This simple tackle is completed by a Clements boom which incorporates a link swivel to take the lead. A heavy-duty swivel is positioned between the trace and the reel line.

Baits
The baits used to lure conger are varied, but mackerel and squid rate highest. Mackerel can be fished whole, but are more usually filleted. When conger are feeding well, though, the bait itself, provided it is fresh, seems not to be too important. The skeleton of a mackerel, the frame after the two flank fillets have been removed, can be as effective as the choicer cuts. Herring is a good but rarely available bait, while bream have been pressed into service with success on days when mackerel have proved scarce.

Coalfish and pollack

Coalfish and pollack are two species which, for angling purposes, can be considered together. They are caught by the same techniques, inhabit the same ground, and are both widely distributed around the whole of the shoreline of the British Isles.

Distribution
Coalfish are found further north near Iceland, extend further along the Norwegian coast, and are, therefore, more common in northern waters of the British Isles. As a species, the coalfish is subjected to rather more commercial pressure than its counterpart and as many as 250,000 tons of coalies are taken annually from the sea around the British Isles and further north by the combined European fishing fleets. Massive concentrations of small coalfish, known locally as saithe or billet, are found in the North Sea and at times they prove to be something of a nuisance to the cod anglers of the Yorkshire, Northumberland, and Durham shorelines.

Pollack are usually found close to rocks and reefs and, like coalfish, are predatory, living on sand-eels, mackerel, herring, and anything else small enough and slow enough to be captured and swallowed whole. The wreck fishing boom, though primarily aimed at conger, produced its crop of other species, including large numbers of pollack and coalfish. In fact both national records were shattered in recent years. The coalfish record has climbed almost annually since it was first broken in June 1971, by John Trust, skipper of *Our Unity*. John landed a fish of 26 lb 2 oz to smash a record which until that time had not been seriously challenged for 50 years. Since 1971 that long-standing record has been exceeded many times and in 1973 it jumped over the 30 lb mark for the first time. A. F. Harris caught a coalfish of 30 lb 12 oz from a wreck beyond the Eddystone, off Plymouth. The pollack record soared from 23 lb 8 oz to 25 lb when Roger Hosking got his big fish, again beyond the Eddystone, in January 1972, and, although the record has been expected to fall again, it has remained intact ever since.

Both the record coalfish and pollack were taken by anglers fishing deep-water wrecks and both species have now become a valued sporting fish, particularly during strong tides when it is impossible to anchor up for the traditional conger and ling fishing. Both coalfish and pollack can be caught – and very often are – from anchored boats, but the main effort against the big fish of both species is now carried out in the December to early March period when both species are at maximum weight. Both spawn in the period January to mid-March which means that anglers fishing for the species at that time are likely to have the best chance of smashing a national record. During this period of the winter both species pack into spawning formations in considerable strength in the lower English Channel. Echo-sounder traces reveal vast hordes of the fish around many of the wrecks. The fish do not stay fast to a single wreck but travel around. A wreck empty of both species one day could abound with them 24 hours later.

Tackle and methods

It was the species' known liking for sand-eels which produced the first of the great artificial baits which have proved so successful in wreck fishing situations. Alex Ingram, of St Austell, designed, perfected, and marketed the Redgill lure, a soft, rubbery imitation sand-eel with an ingenious tail which imparts 'life' to the lure as it is drawn through the water. At first ambitious sea anglers made the mistake of fishing with as many as three of these lures at once. The result was often chaotic. It proved impossible to cope with three fish hooked simultaneously – three fish which frequently totalled over 60 lb in weight. The loss of fish and tackle finally induced a more cautious attitude and it is now very rare for anglers to use more than a single lure at any one time. Coalfish are undoubtedly the stronger of the two species and put up a spectacular performance, equal to anything of its size encountered in the sea. Pollack also fight well, even if they do lack the maintained power of their 'cousins'.

Both species are found off the bottom and are usually anywhere between three fathoms from the sea bed to mid-water in the 30 fathoms or more where most wreck fishing is carried out. The fishing technique therefore is to drop the lure to the sea bed quickly and then to retrieve the first 18 feet of line before slowly retrieving and working the lure back to mid-water. At that position the lure is usually then dropped back down to the bottom and the process repeated. But where shoals are very thick it is often possible to hook fish 'on the drop'. The lead plummeting the lure to the bottom suddenly stops falling – a clear indication that a fish has grabbed the lure and is preventing the lead weight from sinking further.

Drift fishing can be fraught with danger. The fish are first located by echo-sounder and the exact position of the shoal in relation to the wreck is noted. The boat is then taken uptide and is allowed to drift across or along the wreck. The superstructure, masts, stays, and staunchions are all potential hazards to tackle and it is quite usual for at least one of every 10 anglers fishing a wreck in this way to lose his terminal tackle every drift. With each set of gear – lure, Clements boom, weight, and swivel – now costing rather more than £1 a time this can prove an expensive pastime (see figure 16).

Both species can be taken on heavy metal pirks which weigh

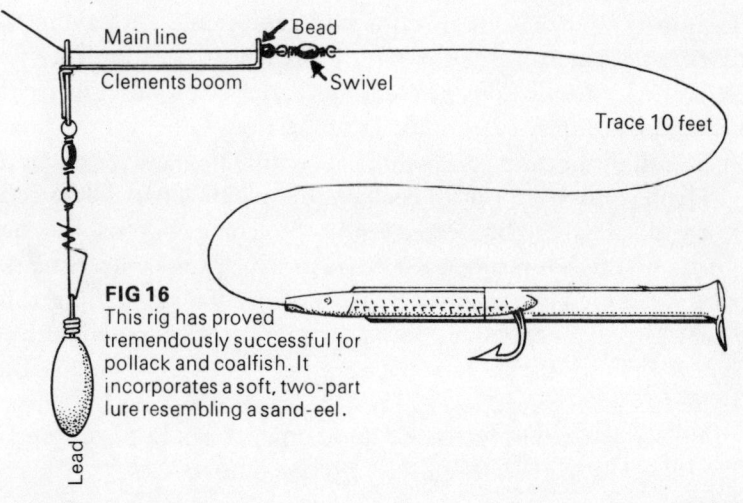

FIG 16
This rig has proved tremendously successful for pollack and coalfish. It incorporates a soft, two-part lure resembling a sand-eel.

as much as 2 lb each – and cost considerably more! Lure fishing with imitation sand-eels is, though, the most sporting and satisfying method. The imitation sand-eels are fished on long traces to obtain more movement and action for the bait. The normal trace is unweighted and is around 10 feet long. In the early days Red Gill sand-eels were armed with relatively small hooks but it became necessary to fit them with much heavier, stronger hooks. Stainless steel models size 8/0 are now standard for wreck fishing, where it is rare to catch either pollack or coalfish weighing less than 10 lb each.

The winter of 1974–75 proved a relative disappointment to coalfish and pollack enthusiasts. The biggest pollack recorded weighed 23 lb 8 oz and the best coalie 28 lb 12 oz, but the national records were never seriously in danger. Much of the blame for this was placed on the vast shoals of sprats, pilchards, and mackerel which accumulated off the south Devon and Cornish coasts. With so much easy feeding within range it was hardly surprising that the pollack and 'coalies' should display less interest in artificials!

It appears, however, that there may have been a more deep-seated reason for this decrease in sport. Catches in the following two seasons continued to disappoint and to this day the promise of the early 1970s has not been fully realised.

Wrecking provides fishing for both species with its big fish and its impact, but there is also much fun to be enjoyed fishing for both species in inshore situations. Pollack are to be found around most rocky headlands, where they can be taken on light tackle using small lures. Natural baits such as ragworm can be float-fished off the bottom successfully at favourable stages of the tide.

Dense concentrations of coalfish, frequently small fish weighing 3 lb or less, can be located within close range of most Scottish ports and this has resulted in a trend in which anglers have fished three feathered hooks among the shoals to win sea angling contests. This is 'easy' fishing in that the fish are willing enough to be caught and it leads to some very heavy contest weights. But there has been a reaction against this type of fishing in competitions on the grounds that it deters anglers from bottom-fishing for bigger, and therefore more worthwhile, species.

Ling

This species is generally found in the same ground and situations as conger eels and the growth of wreck fishing has led to very heavy catches in recent years. To some extent ling is a downgraded species since it is usually taken by anglers fishing for other fish and, while they can put up a good scrap, they are not so highly regarded.

Distribution

The biggest concentrations of ling appear to be in the southernmost sections of the English Channel, particularly southwest of Falmouth. Offshore wrecks in this area seem to contain twice as many ling as wrecks further up-Channel and have at least partially displaced the conger.

The ling record set up in 1912 off Penzance by H. C. Nicholl stood for 62 years before finally going down in 1974. That year a large number of exceptional fish were taken, topped by a massive 50 lb 8 oz specimen by B. Cooper while fishing beyond the Eddystone off Plymouth. And even that fish has been beaten by the 57 lb 2½ oz specimen boated by Henry Solomons off Mevagissey, Cornwall, in 1975. Forty-pound ling are now being taken with increased frequency and it is by no means certain that the present record fish will retain its placing for long. Knowledgeable sea anglers believe the record will one day top 70 lb. Ling taken close inshore tend to be very much smaller than those caught further out in deep water, the south west tip of Cornwall being the exception – but there the sea is much deeper.

Ling are a species with a preference for rocky and very rough ground. Those found in the North Sea tend to be small, but the fish are bigger in Scottish waters and around Shetland, Orkney, and the Hebrides. A 40-pounder has yet to be caught in Scottish waters but fish weighing as much as 35 lb 12 oz have been landed so it could well be that the bigger ones are there awaiting location. The biggest catches of English Channel ling are made from an anchored boat from depths of 30 fathoms or more. Ling are fast to take a bait and can be fished almost to extinction on wrecks. Catches of 1,000 lb of ling have been made over one wreck in a single day. The fish will average nearly 24 lb each, with the occasional 30-pounder but there are so many ling and they feed so greedily by comparison with conger that they have never been highly rated.

Tackle and methods
Ling will happily take a half-mackerel bait offered on a 10/0 hook and it may be that at least some of their failure to become a popular species relates to the fact that they are often caught on heavy tackle intended for conger. In that situation they can hardly be expected to show their best.

Ling can be taken by drift fishing and that is the method generally applied in Scottish waters, where there is, in any case, a marked reluctance to anchor. But drift fishing for ling can be equally costly on tackle as the same type of fishing for halibut. The ground is rough and rock-strewn and, although the bait can be successfully fished off the bottom, it is not possible to anticipate shelves of rock and to avoid the consequent loss of terminal tackle.

Skates and rays

The general heading skates and rays takes in a large number of fish, some of which are regularly caught on rod and line and others which are rarely taken, and then usually only by accident. Their flattened bodies resemble the shape of the flat-fish, though the latter are flattened from side to side and the former are flattened so that they swim on their bellies. They are generally much larger than the flat-fish like flounders and plaice, and have 'wings' – well-developed pectoral fins – and long, whip-like tails.

Though there are many fish in the skates and rays category, it is not necessary to delve deeply into the life history of the various species in what is essentially an angling book. Suffice it to say that they all belong to the same scientific family. The British Record (rod-caught) Fish Committee recognises 12 fish in this family and each of these will be dealt with, with particular emphasis being given to those taken regularly by anglers.

COMMON SKATE
This is the largest of the family. According to Michael Kennedy (in his book *The Sea Angler's Fishes*), it grows to 400 lb. The British Record stands at 226 lb 8 oz and was set up in Shetland waters by Robin MacPherson in 1970. Common skate swim virtually all around our coast in a wide range of depths down to 200 fathoms. They prefer rough areas of sea bed where they feed on a large variety of fish such as smaller skate, dogfish, mackerel, and flatties, as well as crustaceans.

Their tremendous size and strength makes them very popular with anglers and the hard core of common skate hunters is growing every year. Pulling a big skate off the sea bed is one of the greatest challenges left in angling. By its sheer weight and the suction of its large surface area to hug the bottom, the skate can become almost immovable, and, even when the angler succeeds in getting his fish off the bottom, the fight is far from over. It will flap its powerful wings with considerable effect and, if it is a big skate, will often make repeated dives to the bottom.

Distribution

As explained, the common skate can be found all along the British coastline. But there are certain hotspots which produce almost all of the very big skate. The main areas are the waters around the Scottish Highlands and Islands and off the coast of Ireland. Of these two the northern waters have emerged as the best in recent years. Ullapool, on Scotland's west coast, and further north, the islands of Orkney and Shetland, are relatively newly-discovered fishing centres with everything to offer: an abundance of prolific fishing ground, much of it virgin; good facilities; and most important of all, big skate. Those marks already well tried and tested are also thick with coalfish, pollack, haddock, cod, and dogfish. The British record for halibut, bluemouth, megrim, spotted ray, torsk, and common skate all came from these waters. Even shark have been captured in nets.

But the skate which roam these deep waters are without doubt the biggest single attraction to anglers who travel from all over Britain to fish for them. Of the 25 biggest skate caught around the British Isles up to 1973, no less than 23 came from Shetland, Ullapool, Scapa Flow, Stornoway, or Loch Ewe in the Hebrides – all centres in the Highland and Islands Development Board area. And, since MacPherson took his record off Whalsay Island in August 1970, Shetland has become the most popular common skate ground of them all.

The tremendous growth of interest in skate fishing in the north started at Ullapool, in Wester Ross, where the first big skate fell to rod and line in 1961. Lithuanian angler J. Kontrimas started the ball rolling that year with skate of 192 lb and 175 lb. There were heavier fish to come. Twelve skate of more than 100 lb were recorded in 1965, 14 in 1967, and 15 in 1969. Admittedly the pace has slackened since then, but northern waters continue to lead the big skate race. *Angling Times* files list nine 100 lb-plus skate reported in 1973 including two over 200 lb, and eight the following year.

While the skate fishing standard was maintained at centres like Ullapool and Scapa Flow, Orkney and Shetland set higher standards. In 1970 an incredible 75 fish topping 100 lb were landed off Shetland – including MacPherson's record, a 205 lb specimen by Shetland ASA secretary Cavy Johnson, and a 199 lb fish by Lerwick angler J. Goodlad. Shetland continued to improve with between 75 and 80 skate recorded in 1971. The best Shetland fish of that year scaled 187 lb and was caught by Dave Pottinger, another Lerwick angler, off Bard Head. Stornoway produced a 185 lb skate, Orkney a 184 lb specimen, and Ullapool a 175 lb fish.

In 1972, Saltcoats, Ayrshire, angler Bill Currie sounded a reminder that the record was far from intact by taking a 204 lb 8 oz skate during the Shetland Skate Championships. There is no doubt that fish far bigger than the record are swimming in these northern waters, almost certainly in Irish waters too. Many areas of potentially good skate fishing, particularly around Shetland, are still largely unexplored and, as more and more anglers flock to these sea angling playgrounds each year, we can expect to see more and bigger skate being caught (see figure 17).

Tackle and methods

Catching common skate requires very sturdy tackle indeed. The rod is of the utmost importance, for it must be powerful enough to haul the skate from the sea bed, a task made extremely difficult by the very shape of these fish. Imagine trying to pull a giant saucer through the water and you will begin to get the picture. A rod of the type used for shark fishing will fit the bill and, as with shark rods, it is best to have roller rings throughout to minimise friction during what usually turns out to be a long battle.

A large capacity multiplier is the best reel for the job, preferably one with an independently revolving spool. Life can be very dangerous when the reel handle spins with the spool, for the spinning handle can easily break a finger as the fish tears off with the line. The spool, which must be strong enough not to be crushed by the extreme pressure which will be applied when heaving a skate towards the surface, should be loaded with 60 lb

FIG 17
Main skate fishing areas

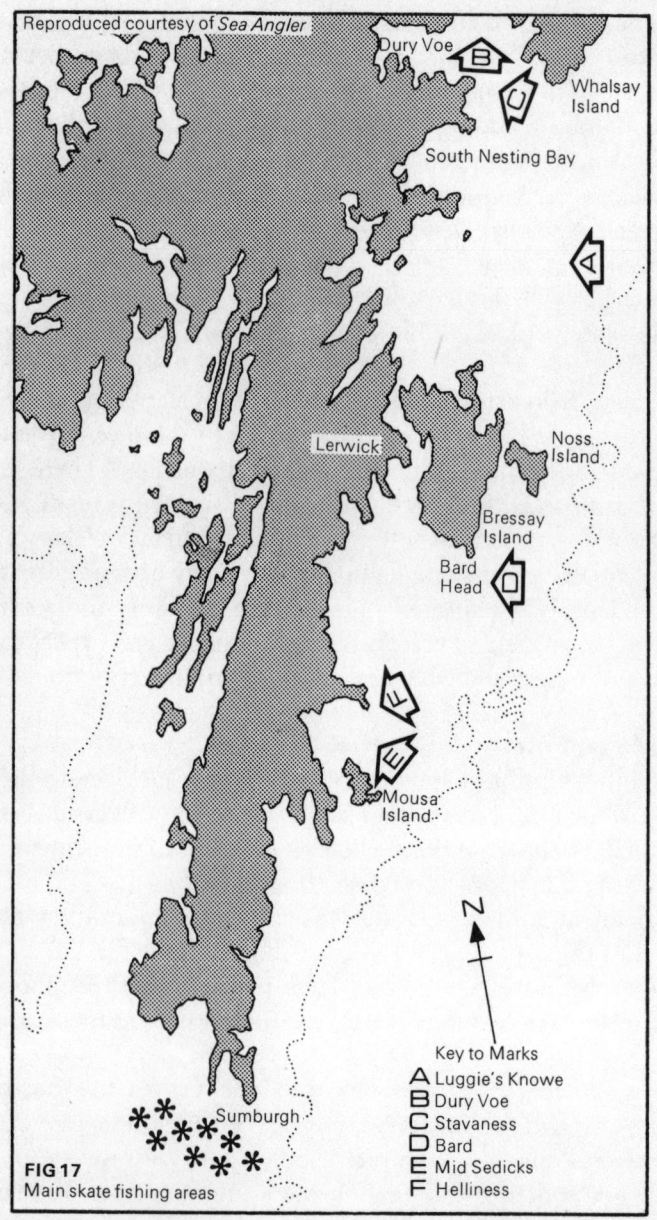

Key to Marks
A Luggie's Knowe
B Dury Voe
C Stavaness
D Bard
E Mid Sedicks
F Helliness

Shetland has emerged as a 'Mecca' for anglers in pursuit of the giant common skate. The 226½ lb British record came from these waters and skate over 100 lb are common. The map illustrates the most productive big-skate grounds. The record fish was caught at Dury Voe.

to 80 lb line. Remember that skate over 100 lb are fairly common.

Large, strong hooks are essential. Small or weak hooks may be straightened by the immense pressure applied on them. A size 10/0 is big enough to take a large bait and to find a secure hold in the skate's powerful jaws. A simple running leger and wire trace is all that is required at the business end of the tackle. Wire is essential because of the skate's deadly teeth and the trace must be at least three feet long to ensure that the fish's rough skin does not chafe and weaken the line above (see figure 18).

Baits

Mackerel is the number one skate bait. A generous offering is required and a whole side of mackerel or the complete fish are the usual offerings. Skate browse along the sea bed in search of their food and never seem to be in a hurry to take a bait. They feed naturally by dropping down on top of a bait and this may give an early indication of a skate's presence. But it is pointless to strike at this point. Give the skate time to get the bait well into its mouth and to move off with it before setting the hook. It is then that the real battle begins.

The aim is to get the skate off the bottom, and even when this is accomplished the fish may dive for the bottom again. This can

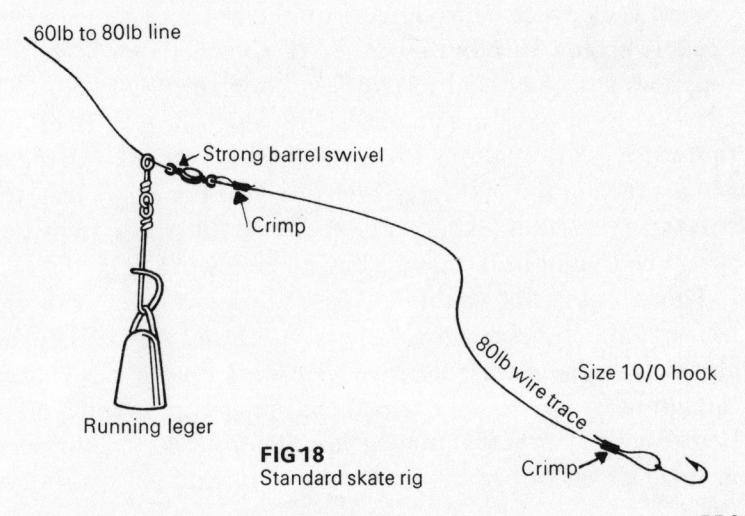

FIG 18
Standard skate rig

occur a number of times, depending on the size of the fish. But the fish gets weaker as time goes on and will eventually succumb to constant pressure. Do not forget that a shoulder harness and butt pad are essential for playing a big skate.

Big skate are usually boated with the aid of two gaffs, one for each wing. Once the fish is swung aboard stay well clear of those powerful jaws and long tail. The jaws are easily capable of crushing a man's hand and the hook should never be removed while the skate is alive.

THORNBACK RAY

The thornback – so called because of the line of spines along its back and tail – is the ray most often caught by anglers. Like the common skate, it is to be found all along our coastline. It is not as big, and the boat record is held by a 38 lb fish caught off Rustington, Sussex, in 1935. The shore record stands at 19 lb, a specimen landed by A. Paterson from Scotland's Mull of Galloway.

Distribution

Known as roker on some parts of the coast, thornback generally run in the 10 lb to 15 lb range, but fish over 20 lb are not rare. Few specimens over 30 lb have been recorded in recent years. One of the best came from Morecambe in Lancashire – a particularly prolific area for the species – in October 1974. That fish weighed 31 lb 8 oz and fell to Fleetwood skipper Frank Bee. The Welsh coast is also a good area for these fish. A 31 lb 6¾ oz thornback was caught at Rhyl in March 1970 and a party of anglers fishing the same area later that year boated 42 fish, the best weighing 18 lb. Another good Welsh fish was a 32 lb 4 oz specimen caught in Barmouth Bay the following year.

Though basically a summer species, good catches of thornback are sometimes taken as early as March and April. They can also be caught in their deep water haunts during the winter, though most anglers are normally too preoccupied with cod to bother with them at that time of year. Thornbacks tend to swim in small shoals of perhaps only a dozen or less fish which feed on the bottom. Their diet includes small flat-fish, whiting, crustaceans, and worms.

Tackle and methods
Thornbacks will fight reasonably well on light tackle, using their flat, disc-like shape to full advantage in the tide. A light, eight-foot boat rod coupled with a small multiplier loaded with 12 lb line will bring the best out of them. The time for catching thornbacks coincides with the tope season and it is not unlikely that a stray tope will bring added excitement to a day's thornback fishing, especially on such light tackle.

Terminal tackle should be kept simple. As with many other types of fishing, the simplest rigs are often the most effective. A running leger is all that is needed, although it is wise to use a wire link between line and hook. Thornbacks do not have such powerful teeth as common skate but their boney jaws and rough lips can weaken ordinary line. Considering the bait is likely to be a fish strip or a chunky piece of squid, a size 6/0 hook is a good choice.

BLONDE RAY
This species of ray is less widespread than the thornback and the common and is only large enough in numbers for angling purposes off the south coast and in the Irish Sea. It is very scarce in the North Sea.

Blonde ray prefer soft ground and the sandy banks, which are good for turbot and plaice, are also excellent fishing grounds. The Shambles Bank off Weymouth, Dorset, is a definite hotspot. For example, in 1974, specimens of 34 lb 11 oz, 29 lb 8 oz, and 28 lb 8 oz were taken there. The boat record weighed 37 lb 12 oz when caught by Salcombe, Devon, angler Harry Pout off Start Point, Devon, in 1973. Other good grounds include the Varne Bank off the Kent Coast, the Skerries Bank off the Devon coast, and certain areas off Jersey in the Channel Islands. It was in fact a Channel Islands mark which produced the 25 lb 4 oz shore record for S. Sangan. He fished from Greve de Lecq Pier, Jersey.

The blonde ray, which does not have the spines of the thornback, feeds mainly on worms, sand-eels, and crustaceans, but it is usually caught on strips of fish.

STING RAY

The sting ray is one of the rarer, but larger, of its family. It has been caught at various points in the Channel, usually by anglers fishing for other types of fish. The British record stands at 59 lb and those caught on rod and line are rarely below 40 lb. The Sussex coast appears to have a particular attraction to sting ray if recent rod and line catches are anything to go by. A 48 lb fish was caught off Seaford in 1971, a 55-pounder off Selsey in 1972, and fish of 49 lb and 52 lb by the same angler off Littlehampton in 1974. All these fish, plus a 60-pounder speared off Shoreham in 1969, were caught in the summer months.

Domination by the Sussex coast is broken by the current shore record, a 51 lb 4 oz sting-ray caught from Sowley Beach, Hampshire, by A. Stevens in 1975.

It is, as its name implies, a dangerous fish. The long tail is armed with a spine which carries a dangerous venom. This venom causes temporary paralysis at best and can be fatal. Understandably many anglers chop the tail off as soon as the fish is caught.

SMALL-EYED RAY

The small-eyed ray owes a lot to a certain Harry Pout, who also holds the blonde ray record. A pensioner living at Salcombe, Devon, Harry brought the species into the public eye with a series of exceptional catches off his local shoreline. He does, in fact, hold the British boat record with a 16 lb 4 oz specimen he caught in September 1973. He had also broken the record a month earlier with a fish weighing just an ounce under 14 lb. The area where Harry caught his fish is certainly a hotspot. Another Salcombe angler caught a brace of small-eyed ray weighing 13 lb 7 oz and 13 lb 4 oz on the same grounds.

Small-eyed ray are fairly common in the Channel though they are often mistaken for other species of ray. Few anglers fish especially for small-eyed ray and they are usually caught by accident. One of the few areas where they are fished for intentionally is around the Isle of Wight. Most small-eyed ray are caught from boats but in this area they are taken from the shore. Catches have been recorded from numerous marks around the Island but the best ground is to be found along the southern shores between St Catherine's and Compton Bay where there is a contrast between gently shelving beaches and beaches which drop off quickly to a depth of 30 to 40 feet.

The rocky ledges further offshore keep the trawlers at bay and the small-eyed ray move in quite large shoals. Island experts advocate a light beachcaster, a trace of about 18 lb and a 5/0 or 6/0 hook baited with sand-eel. Other good baits include fish strips, squid, ragworm, and cuttlefish. The best terminal rig is a simple one-hook paternoster. The Isle of Wight shore record stands at 11 lb 8 oz and the boat record at 15 lb 14 oz.

SPOTTED RAY

Another of the 'middle order' rays, this species has been caught to a weight of 6 lb 3 oz 4 dr. That boat-caught fish was caught by P. England off the Isle of Mull, Scotland, in 1977. The shore record of 7 lb 12 oz is held by P. Dower with a fish taken in 1977 at Plymouth. It is found all around our coasts but does not figure prominently in anglers' catches. It is found on the same type of ground as the blonde ray and is often confused with this fish. The more prominent snout of the spotted ray is its most distinguishing feature.

UNDULATE RAY

The West Country, Sussex, and Channel Island coasts appear to be the best areas for this member of the ray family but again it is not a species often caught on rod and line. The British boat record of 19 lb 6 oz 13 dr was taken off Herm in the Channel Islands in 1970. A previous record fish of 10 lb 10¼ oz also came from Channel Island waters two years earlier. The shore record stands at 10 lb 10¼ oz.

SANDY RAY
This is one of the smaller rays. It is found in depths of up to about 150 fathoms and is mainly an offshore species. The Record Fish Committee is awaiting claims at a minimum weight of 4 lb.

ELECTRIC OR TORPEDO RAY
This is not a fish often encountered by the angler but it is recognised by the British Record (rod-caught) Fish Committee at a weight of 96 lb 1 oz. That fish was caught off Dodman Point, Cornwall, but so few are taken on rod and line that nowhere can they be said to be common. We do know they prefer the sea bed to be soft in moderate depths and that their food consists chiefly of other fish such as flatties, gurnard, and eels. They catch other fish by stunning them with an electrical charge from 'batteries' in their pectoral fins, hence their name.

These batteries are concentrations of jelly-filled cells. The upper side of the fish is the positive electrode and the lower side the negative electrode. The sea water completes the circuit. An angler who touches both sides of a freshly-caught electric ray at the same time is likely to get quite a jolt. Fortunately these fish are easily identified. For while most skates and rays have pointed noses, this fish is cut square across the front. Electric rays are known to attain a weight of more than 100 lb.

EAGLE RAY
This fish has been found along various parts of our coasts, including the Channel, and the North, and Irish Seas, but it is rarely caught by anglers. Identified by a long slender tail, it has a blunt head and sharply pointed wings. The British boat record is 52 lb 8 oz, a fish caught off the Isle of Wight in 1972. The shore record is awaiting claims at 25 lb.

CUCKOO RAY
This is the smallest of the rays to be found off the British coastline and is very similar in appearance to the sandy ray. The cuckoo does, however, have the longer tail of the two and the snout is not so pointed. Found all around our coasts, it swims in shallow and moderate depths feeding on worms, sand-eels, and crusta-

ceans. The 5 lb 11 oz boat record was caught off Ireland's Causeway Coast in 1975. The shore record awaits claims at 4 lb 8 oz.

BOTTLE-NOSED RAY OR WHITE SKATE
Often referred to as white skate because of its white belly, this fish is the largest of all the skates and rays. Though the British boat record is held with a fish of only 76 lb, it may attain a weight of up to 500 lb. The heaviest recorded on rod and line was a 165-pounder taken at Clew Bay, County Mayo, in 1966. It has been caught in northern waters but is usually more southern in its distribution than the common skate and is normally caught during the warmer months. A 110 lb specimen was boated off the Needles mark near the Isle of Wight but the fish was hooked in the tail and did not qualify as a British record. The present record was, incidentally, taken from the same waters in 1970. Like the common skate, it feeds on other fish and crustaceans. It derives the name bottle-nosed ray from the distinctive shape of its snout.

Halibut

It is only comparatively recently that fishing for halibut with rod and line has become a matter to be taken seriously. For centuries, long-line fishermen have taken halibut in northern waters – Shetland, Orkney and around the far tip of the Scottish mainland. But only now is there any sign of a major effort with rod and line.

The halibut closely resembles an out-sized flounder, and the British rod-caught record currently stands at 212 lb 4 oz and was taken by J. Hewitt off Dunnet Head, Scotland, in 1975 – but far bigger fish have yet to be caught in this area. British trawlers fishing the distant grounds have returned to port with halibut weighing in excess of 400 lb, and 500-pounders must be a possibility in the near future. It is, of course, open to doubt if these leviathans are found within striking distance of the British Isles. Long-liners never recorded the upper limit weights of the fish they caught. It seems a reasonable assumption that, while the record can be expected to be pushed upwards at any time, it may take many years before we see the first 300-pounder on rod and line.

Distribution

Halibut range along the Irish Atlantic seaboard and it was from this coast, particularly off County Kerry that the first rod and line halibut began to show. A number of fish topping the 100 lb mark were taken between the wars before catches lost their impetus and became much more spasmodic. On the other hand, halibut fishing in Highland and Island waters made little progress until after the Second World War. Even by the beginning of 1975 less than 40 halibut had been taken from British home waters on rod and line but the stimulus is there. Oddly enough, one of the prime boosts for halibut fishing came as a result of an *Angling Times* halibut fishing sortie to Iceland. Heavy publicity for the first trip and others that followed since, have whetted the public appetite, inspired by the big fish taken in Iceland's Breidafjordur, a shallow bay on the island's west coast.

It may yet prove that the West of Scotland grounds are also potentially sound halibut fishing areas. When rod and line fishing builds up out from Skye and the Outer Hebrides outstanding results could follow. Halibut do occasionally move much further south and there is at least one confirmed trawler catch in the lower section of the English Channel. It remains true though that these fish are stragglers from the main holding areas and rod and line fishing other than on the west coast of Ireland and in Scottish waters is likely to be very poorly rewarded.

Tackle and methods

With a great deal still remaining to be discovered about halibut – their migratory habits, feeding patterns, and rate of growth – it is best not to adopt too dogmatic an approach to the species. Sufficient to say that the Scottish long-liners expect their first fish in April and catches continue until the autumn. As a general rule these long lines are baited with fish which, by the standards anglers apply to rod and line fishing, are none too fresh. Perhaps this does not matter. The fish could be scavengers, but they are also known to like sand-eels and to feed very heavily on crabs and lobsters.

It was not until the Icelandic halibut fishing had been sampled that the myth that 200 lb halibut were so strong they would prove impossible to beat on rod and line was exploded. In fact, the Breidafjordur's halibut are quite sluggish fish. The bite itself is gentle and the fish are slow to move. It seems a logical assumption that since the Breidafjordur is in part nearly barren of food fish – and that part contains large numbers of halibut – the fish in fact feed almost entirely on shellfish. It follows that since crabs and lobsters are slow-moving the halibut has no need to hurry when picking up its food. The absence of tide makes matters easier for the angler and it has so far proved that, as long as he is capable of maintaining contact with even the biggest of the fish while they undertake their series of characteristic dives from the surface to the bottom, then success will not be far away.

The halibut come to the surface quite easily when first hooked but fish weighing 50 lb and more suddenly accelerate, change direction, and zoom to the sea bed at maximum speed. It follows that the clutch of the angler's multiplier reel should not be set too tight or sudden impact from the diving fish will tear the hook out of its mouth. Inspection of a halibut's mouth shows its resemblance to an over-grown flounder. The sides of the mouth are quite fragile and this emphasises the importance of playing the fish on a lightly-set clutch. At most even the biggest halibut are unlikely to dive more than five times and, provided the angler keeps his hookhold intact, he retains every chance of winning the encounter. This theory gains support from the fact that halibut over 100 lb have been landed on relatively frail tackle. There are instances both in Icelandic and British water of fish being beaten on light lines and size 1/0 hooks by anglers 'feathering' for small fish.

Most halibut are hooked on the drift. The boat is allowed to move across the sea with the anglers' baits trailing along, either on or very close to the sea bed. Since halibut are often contacted over rough if not downright rocky ground this can lead to the loss of excessive amounts of terminal tackle. A slow drift seems best, but since halibut take the bait without dashing away immediately afterwards, it is sometimes difficult to be sure whether it is the sea bed or a fish providing the weight on the rod top.

In the summer of 1974 a group of Bradford anglers spent a week fishing the deep-water section of the Pentland Firth, where charts show 42 fathoms of water. They proved their point that this wild, dangerous tide-rip between Caithness and Orkney holds above average numbers of halibut by hooking four good fish. Unfortunately all were lost, although one big one was on top of the water at one stage of the battle. It was lost with the halibut's characteristic rocket-like return to the sea bed. It has to be said that a halibut hooked in a strong tide represents a much more difficult prospect than fish taken from slack water. When broadside to the current the fish have the flow for an ally and the combination of fish and current can lead to the hook tearing out of the fish's mouth.

Anglers are still in the process of learning how best to fish for halibut, but it now seems there is no need for extra-strong tackle. A 50 lb breaking strain line seems adequate, allied to a multiplier reel fitted with a smooth clutch which concedes line as required at the crucial stages of the battle. An over-stiff rod could be a disadvantage. When these fish change direction at speed it is vital that there should be enough movement in the rod to minimise the impact felt from the fish, thus reducing the pressure on the hookhold. Halibut do not toy with a bait. They move close to it and with one effective suck draw the bait into their mouths. In other words the bait is there, and then a split second later it has disappeared into the fish. Due to the halibut's fragile mouth, it seems wise to give the fish time to take the bait deep down before striking. For a fish hooked in the lower throat is less likely to throw the hook. It follows that a big hook is better than a small one, but bearing in mind that some 100 lb-plus halibut have been landed on relatively tiny hooks, the hookhold itself must be the most crucial factor.

Halibut have been taken on pirks, those heavy lures fitted with treble hooks which are jigged, often with bait on the hooks, in the lower section of the sea. They have also been taken on mackerel feathers and on whole fish baits being offered for common skate. So one needs only to be fishing in a good area to have a chance of hooking a halibut – almost regardless of the method being used.

For all that, fishing for these king-size flat-fish can be a dour business, costly in both time and terminal tackle and often frustrating in the extreme. A full week's fishing can produce not so much as a single bite. Yet the halibut is fast emerging as perhaps the greatest challenge remaining in the seas lapping the British shoreline. Of all the fish available only mako shark and tunny grow bigger and they are with us only fleetingly and in very small numbers.

Pouting

Love them or hate them, you just cannot ignore pouting. These attractive little fish play an important part in competition fishing on the south coast where they can be caught in prolific numbers to build up a high winning weight. But they are much maligned by pleasure fishermen who are troubled by their bait-pinching habits when bigger fish are the quarry. Pouting are with us all the year round. They can be caught from beach, boat and pier and you do not have to be an expert to catch them. The average pouting weighs from 1 lb to 2 lb.

Boat fishing is the most productive method. Pouting do move in along the beaches but these tend to be the smaller fish. A lot of undersized pouting are caught from the shore during spring and summer and it is the autumn months which provide the best chance of better fish in the 2 lb class.

Beach fishing is best after dark when pouting tend to come in much closer and feed more voraciously. This is the case not only when beach fishing but also from pier and boat. Pouting are a bottom feeding fish. They stick to the two or three feet of water closest to the sea bed and rarely swim high enough in the sea to make floatfishing a serious proposition. A long trace with two hooks above the weight provides sufficiently attractive movement in the tide and is a favourite method from beach and pier.

But 'pouting snatching' really comes into its own when boat fishing. Any novice can catch pouting, but taking them at a rate fast enough to win a competition is an art in itself. It takes an experienced man to do it properly.

The Kent coast between Deal and Folkestone is probably the most prolific pouting ground around the coast. Here the anglers favour a three hook trace and place great importance on putting a swivel on each hook. For one of the curses of pouting fishing is that in a strong tide a hooked fish will spin in the water, kinking and twisting the line.

The type of trace used varies according to the tide. In a moderately slack tide a paternoster trace with one hook below the weight and two above will do the job. Use the hooks on wire booms which hold them clear of the line and eliminate tangles. Remember, you don't have to cast from a boat. Just lower the rig over the side. Alternatively two hooks can be positioned below the weight and one above. The choice of hook arrangement depends on the colour of the water. Pouting tend to venture that little bit farther from the sea bed when the water is clear, but they will hug the bottom in a murky sea. Generally speaking the bigger fish are taken on the hooks below the weight because they have a tendency to swim closer to the bottom. As with bass, the smaller fish in a pouting shoal tend to swim above the bigger ones.

Different tactics are required for dead slack water. The spreader paternoster has been largely written off by many people in the sea angling world but it is still a fine piece of tackle. The advantage is that the wire booms are spread so that the tackle cannot tangle on the way down. It can plummet down to the bottom as fast as the weight can carry it with no fear of tangling.

If you are fishing a competition and speed is important do not use large portions of bait. Pouting are an obliging fish and will greedily accept the tiniest offering. They will also take whatever you care to throw at them. Pieces of worm, herring strip and razorfish are all good baits and squid is often particularly good for the bigger specimens.

Pouting bait does not have to be absolutely fresh but it pays to use a piece of fresh lugworm on at least one of the hooks to keep the shoal interested. It is also a useful ploy to bait one of the hooks with razorfish. This is a tougher bait and alleviates the need to rebait all of the hooks on every cast.

Pouting cannot be caught so quickly in a fast tide. Under these conditions a long three-hook trace is the answer, the trace providing extra attraction by its movement in the tide.

Whichever rig is being used it is a good idea to continually bounce the lead by jerking the rod top. This will add movement to the baits and this will draw the pouting.

It is almost impossible to hook a pouting on its first knock at the bait. Therefore it is necessary to give the fish a couple of yards of slack line. This will give the eager fish plenty of time to get the bait well into its mouth so that the angler is virtually certain to contact on the strike. Good competition anglers use hooks small enough for pouting but big enough to hold a cod if one should come along. A 1/0 will do the job nicely.

During the settled weather, the likely spots to look for pouting are in the rocks and around the wrecks. But rough seas drive them out on to smoother ground. It could be that there is more food available on the smooth ground after a good blow. Although pouting are with us all year round, they do not like very cold temperatures. In cold weather they will move off the shallow beaches into the deeper water where they can still be caught by boat anglers.

Most anglers do not appreciate the fighting qualities of the pouting. This is because they are usually caught on baits and tackle intended for bigger species such as cod. But tackle them with an eight-foot hollow fibre glass boat rod, 11 lb line, a light weight and a single hook and you will discover just what a handful a 3 lb pouting can be. The pouting itself is a strikingly handsome fish. Those caught inshore are a silvery colour with pink stripes across the back, while pouting caught in deeper water, particularly over wrecks, have gold flanks and jet black stripes.

The biggest pouting on record weighed 5 lb 8 oz and was boated by R. S. Armstrong off Berry Head, Devon, in 1969. The British Record Fish Committee do not include a shore record on their list at this time. They are awaiting claims at a minimum qualifying weight of 3 lb.

DISCARDED AND SOLD